MAKING DISCIPLES

APPLYING TRUTH IN DAILY LIVING

carla maclachlan

Published by Bound by Faith Publishers
www.boundbyfaithpublishers.com

ISBN: 978-0-9829029-5-0 · Ebook ISBN: 978-0-9829029-6-7

Printed in the United States of America

I am forever grateful for the support, encouragement, and, most of all, the many prayers of family members and friends throughout this endeavor. I would especially like to thank Mandy Zerwig who has worked with me in ministry for many years. Her dedication and diligence in helping me communicate truth accurately and effectively was a labor of love unto the Lord.

To God be the glory.

CONTENTS

INTRODUCTION

If you were going to offer help to someone, in which environment would you experience more confidence: one that is familiar or unfamiliar? We're often more comfortable and confident serving from an environment that is personally familiar because we know what is accessible to us, where things are located, and how to use what is available. In this same way, God wants us to become comfortable and confident with each step of the process of making disciples—comfortable using His Word and fully confident in His power to achieve His purpose.

Acts 17:28 teaches that it's in Christ that believers live and move and have their being. As you learn to operate in your true identity and position in Christ, you will become increasingly comfortable operating under God's authority and in His strength. The Bible will become increasingly familiar as you consistently equip yourself with truth through the study of God's Word. As a result, you will have more confidence to disciple others. *Making Disciples* will equip you to personally walk according to biblical truth and to train others to do the same.

Because a person can never take someone further than he is willing to go himself, choose to use this book to first apply truth in your own life before considering its use in the lives of others. Ask the Holy Spirit to reveal Himself to you through the use of Scripture and to enable you to implement each biblical principle that is presented. In doing so, you will become a living example of Jesus for others to follow, enabling you to make disciples as God commands.

CHAPTERS 1 AND 2

THE SIGNIFICANCE OF DISCIPLESHIP

CHAPTER ONE

The Basis for Discipleship

To put it simply, a disciple of Jesus is someone who chooses to believe in, learn from, and follow Him. Discipleship is a process by which believers are taught biblical principles and how to apply them in practical ways. The idea of making disciples is found in the Bible, the Word of God.

In Matthew 28:18–20, Jesus gave instructions to His followers. Many people now refer to these instructions as the Great Commission: *Then Jesus came to them and said, "All authority in heaven and earth has been given to me. Therefore go and make disciples of all nations, baptizing them in the name of the Father and of the Son and of the Holy Spirit, and teaching them to obey everything I have commanded you. And surely I am with you always, to the very end of the age."* Up until this point in His ministry, Jesus' twelve disciples had stayed near Him both in physical proximity and relationship. They had followed Jesus closely, learning from His example.

At this time, Jesus was sending them out to share with others the truth He had so fervently instilled in them. It would not be long before the disciples would receive the indwelling Holy Spirit, which would supernaturally empower them to do all the things Jesus had asked of them. Through this abiding relationship with His Spirit, Christ would always be with them. How amazing it is to realize that today we, too, have the truth of Christ Jesus and the enabling power of the Holy Spirit available to us. Therefore, we also have the potential to successfully make disciples of others.

So, how does one convert potential into actuality? Think about this: When a person is considered for employment, two things are consistently brought into question—education and experience. These components are important in tandem because a person who has knowledge, coupled with application, proves to be most efficient and effective in their area of service. The same is true for those serving in the kingdom of God. God gave us the Bible so we can gain knowledge of His instructions. He also provided, through His Son Jesus, a living example of the way His truth is to be successfully applied in our daily lives. In addition, God gives us the indwelling Holy Spirit, empowering us in every way to accomplish His will.

As we continually rely on the knowledge of God's Word and the power of His Spirit, our habits will develop into a lifestyle that mirrors Jesus. This lifestyle, or pattern, of walking according to the truth of God's Word represents a personal path of righteousness. Through the experience of walking righteously, we can then lead others to do the same.

As a result of the personal application of these truths, the apostle Paul became an excellent example of a genuine disciple of Jesus, his words matching his lifestyle and his lifestyle matching the truth of God's Word. Then he made disciples of others by developing in them this same pattern of living. In 1 Corinthians 4:16–17 Paul wrote, *Therefore I urge you to imitate me. For this reason I am sending to you Timothy, my son whom I love, who is faithful in the Lord. He will remind you of my way of life in Christ Jesus, which agrees with what I teach everywhere in every church.*

Paul understood that he could only lead others as well as he was personally following Jesus. Because of his faithful obedience to Jesus, Paul could ask others to imitate him. In doing so, he was asking them to focus on Christ's transforming work in his life. Timothy's spiritual maturity was a result of the work of the Lord and also demonstrated the example and instruction of Paul. As with Paul, we, too, must become genuine imitators of Christ in order to effectively influence others to follow Jesus.

As we progress in becoming faithful followers of Jesus, God will provide opportunities to influence others for His kingdom. It is during these occasions that our quality of preparation will be revealed. Just as we prepare for a career by gaining knowledge and training to be more qualified, we must gain knowledge of God's Word and be experienced in its application in order to more effectively influence others for Christ.

In considering ways to intentionally and purposefully prepare to disciple others, you may find it beneficial to first examine this entire book for practical application of biblical principles. Remember, the best way to develop genuine discipleship in others is to become a living example of Christlikeness for them to follow. For this reason, it is essential to first apply truth in your own life before asserting its use in the lives of others. There may be times throughout this book when you are presented with truths that you're already applying in your life. Rather than skim over these sections, praise God for the work He is accomplishing in you. Then, ask the Lord to reveal any additional lessons He desires for you to glean from each specific principle.

When you encounter biblical truths that are new to you or are currently absent in your life, ask God to enable you to grasp all He desires for you to learn from each precept. Keep in mind that your goal is not to complete this book in a set timeframe, but to establish, practice, and thereby develop as a lifestyle everything God would have you apply from His Word. This means that there may be times when you need to camp on a particular subject to allow God to fully teach you from His Word, and then practically employ it before moving on to another subject. As you allow God to make His truth real and to apply it personally, the pages of Scripture will become alive and useful in your daily life.

Be aware that there may be times in this book when the discussion of a biblical principle may seem repetitive. However, many subjects will be initially covered to consider their importance in personal discipleship, and then later to show application and significance when training others. Ask the Holy Spirit to reveal Himself to you as you read Scripture and then help you implement each biblical principle that is presented. In doing so, you will become a living example of Christ for others to follow, enabling you to disciple them as God commands.

CHAPTER TWO

Criteria for Discipleship

The countless denominations representing the Christian faith and the many different people attending these churches can create confusion for those trying to distinguish a genuine disciple of Jesus. Since discipleship originated with God, it makes sense to rely on His Word, rather than man's word, to define a true disciple. Therefore, in order to identify a present-day disciple of Jesus, we should look at the disciples of Jesus' day. In doing so, we choose to lay down our own perceptions of what a disciple may look like to embrace the criteria used in the Bible.

For example, in the New Testament Jesus personally invited, or called, His disciples. Matthew 9:9 tells us, *As Jesus went on from there, he saw a man named Matthew sitting at the tax collector's booth. "Follow me," he told him, and Matthew got up and followed him.* In Mark 1:17–18, Jesus was walking along the Sea of Galilee when He extended an invitation to Simon and his brother Andrew: *"Come, follow me," Jesus said, "and I will make you fishers of men." At once they left their nets and followed him.*

Just as in biblical times, Jesus still calls people today to follow Him and, in every case, Jesus' invitation to become a disciple requires a response. These verses demonstrate that the response is to be an immediate action of obedience rather than merely verbal assent. Notice that the invitation is "to follow." Jesus never asks us to run ahead of Him or to pursue anything apart from Him. Christ Jesus asks us to follow Him because He knows best how to lead and the direction He wants us to go.

Have you acknowledged and accepted the call from Jesus to follow Him? Have you embraced Christ as your personal Lord by abandoning your own desires to follow His lead, allowing Him to rule in your heart and life? In addition to personal discipleship, Jesus has a greater purpose for His call on our lives—to make us "fishers of men" who effectively convey the truth of Christ to others. Are you willing to allow Jesus to train you to become an effective "fisher of men"?

Similar to other invitations, Scripture teaches that accepting the invitation to become a disciple of Jesus has stipulations. This means that God not only desires certain things from His followers but also has requirements. God asks us to follow His requirements, so that we may experience life's benefits to the fullest, not as a means to control our lives. The things God asks of us may not be easy, but they are necessary for spiritual success. A believer doesn't fully or completely meet Christ's requirements when he initially becomes a disciple of Jesus. Following Jesus is a moment by moment, day by day process of growing in obedience. As we mature in obedience, our lives are transformed to reflect Christ. As a result, God is honored and we reap the benefits (Romans 6:22).

Anyone may call himself a disciple. Some people today are led to believe that followers of Jesus are developed through church attendance, financial giving, and volunteering to help those in need.

Although these are good and may be a product of discipleship, the ultimate goal of discipleship is to become more like Christ Jesus. Therefore, the choice to follow and the manner in which we follow are of extreme significance. In other words, personal discipleship is a deliberate choice that must be Christ-led and Christ-centered to produce the desired outcome of genuine transformation.

The question then becomes this: Can we learn what the process of discipleship should look like and are we committed to the process? The answer to the first part of this question is yes. The Bible clearly shows us what the process of discipleship looks like, and God equips every believer with the Holy Spirit to enable him or her to successfully follow the Holy Spirit's lead. (This will be explained in practical detail in this book.) The second part of the question must be answered by each individual. Are you committed to the process of discipleship?

Discipleship is indeed a lifelong process. However, each step of the process should reflect actions based on biblical truth that will result in a consistent progression toward spiritual maturity. You may want to remember it this way: commitment to the process will produce consistent progress. In the fourth chapter of 1 Timothy, Paul spoke about the devotion and diligence necessary for the process of discipleship. In verse 15 he wrote, *Be diligent in these matters; give yourself wholly to them, so that everyone may see your progress.* Your spiritual progress is a testimony to God's transforming work in your life!

It may be helpful at this point to examine a stipulation for discipleship presented in the Bible and what the transformation process might look like. In Luke 9:23 Jesus said, *"If anyone would come after me, he must deny himself and take up his cross daily and follow me."* (The word *if* often identifies stipulations in the Bible.) In this case, Jesus is explaining what is required of those who would consider following Him.

To truly follow Jesus is not a one-time commitment but a daily resolve to deny oneself for the sake of Christ. In doing so, we consistently put aside personal desires to embrace those things that are most pleasing to God. Just as Jesus became a living example of one who followed God the Father in total commitment, even unto death (Philippians 2:5–8), we, too, are to show the same humble and obedient devotion to our Lord.

As you know, denying self will not come naturally—it will take deliberate intent. Denying self means that you place Jesus and others as a priority over self, being careful to keep the things of this world from coming between you and your relationship with Christ. This may mean that God prompts you to turn off the television to spend more time studying His Word or in prayer for others. The Lord may ask you to give up some personal comfort to serve those in need. Following Jesus may cause you to miss a family dinner because He leads you to share His plan of salvation with a co-worker after work.

As a person consistently chooses to deny himself for the purpose of furthering Christ's kingdom, his life is transformed, increasingly looking more like the perfect servant, Jesus (Mark 10:45). This consistent transformation is spiritually maturing, or progressing in the process of growing in Christ. Although the discipline of denying self will be further examined later, begin asking yourself the following questions to determine its existence in your life: Are you daily choosing to set aside selfish desires to pursue the things of Christ? Are you consistently allowing God's will to override your own?

In Luke 9:23, Jesus used the word *must* to show the requirement for each disciple to deny himself, take up his cross daily, and follow Him. When Jesus tells us to "take up our cross," it's a perfect word picture of complete sacrifice. Just as Jesus willingly sacrificed His life on the cross for the sins of the world, we, too, are to have a willing desire to sacrifice whatever Christ asks of us. Although Jesus may never ask you to sacrifice everything, He does stipulate that His disciples be genuinely willing to do so.

While sacrifice comes in various forms, all of those who choose to follow Jesus will be called to personal sacrifice—to give up things that please self for things that please Him. However, it's assuring to know that Jesus will never ask us to do something without also supernaturally enabling us to do it. Therefore, as you depend on the indwelling power of the Holy Spirit, you will be able to victoriously deny self and triumphantly carry your cross regardless of what that may entail.

These two components of discipleship, denying oneself and taking up one's cross daily, should be clearly understood and carefully considered, since they are written prerequisites to following Jesus. Are you willing to embrace personal sacrifice for the kingdom of Christ? Is there anything in this world that would prevent you from living life sold out to Him?

Paul explained a life sold out to Jesus in 2 Corinthians 5:14–15: *For Christ's love compels us, because we are convinced that one died for all, and therefore all died. And he died for all, that those who live should no longer live for themselves but for him who died for them and was raised again.* Are you willing to surrender control of your life for the sake of following the perfect will of Jesus?

As a result of studying God's Word, we can begin to see what the ongoing process of discipleship looks like: A person must first respond to Jesus' call by acknowledging Him as Savior and Lord (John 1:35–42). Additionally, the person is to abandon earthly pursuits in order to live for Christ's eternal kingdom (Luke 14:33). Also, a genuine disciple will continuously walk in obedience to the Lord and His teaching (John 8:31–32).

In Galatians 2:20 Paul wrote, *I have been crucified with Christ and I no longer live, but Christ lives in me. The life I live in the body, I live by faith in the Son of God, who loved me and gave himself for me.* The life of a Christ-follower is characterized by steady growth in faith and trust, as well as increasing reliance on Jesus. Remember, commitment to the process will produce consistent progress. It's in this state of growing in total dependence on Jesus, emptied of self, that a disciple can best be used of God.

Second Timothy 2:20–21 teaches that those who follow God's directives will become most effective for His kingdom: *In a large house there are articles not only of gold and silver, but also of wood and clay; some are for noble purposes and some for ignoble. If a man cleanses himself from the latter, he will be an instrument for noble purposes, made holy, useful to the Master and prepared to do any good work.*

A disciple is most effective for God's higher, noble purposes, when they become cleansed from the things that disqualify their character. As you surrender your life to Christ by becoming emptied of self, set apart to Him, and pursuant of holiness, you will become a clean vessel; an instrument useful to God, prepared to do His work. As a result, others will recognize your life as one who believes in, learns from, and follows Jesus.

CHAPTERS 3 THROUGH 9

PURPOSEFUL PREPARATION

CHAPTER THREE

The Pursuit of Personal Holiness

When we commit to wholeheartedly following Jesus, we set our lives on a course to pursue righteousness, or holiness, by earnestly seeking those things that reflect Him and His Word. First Peter 1:14–16 tells us, *As obedient children, do not conform to the evil desires you had when you lived in ignorance. But just as he who called you is holy, so be holy in all you do; for it is written: "Be holy, because I am holy."* Jesus calls each of us to a lifestyle that is set apart from the world for His holy purposes. As you may have already experienced, such a lifestyle doesn't occur automatically. It takes place as a result of personal resolve and diligent pursuit.

As with other personal journeys, the same considerations are significant when pursuing the things of God. The direction to take, the means of travel, who and what you should take with you, and the potential cost are all factors that should be well thought through to achieve success along the way. Psalm 18:30 teaches that God's ways are perfect. Since there's nothing better than perfect, it's fitting that we should contemplate God's way of pursuing righteousness. The following questions and answers should assist in doing so.

What route should we take in pursuing holiness?

In pursuing the holiness of God, it's valuable to examine the paths you've already experienced in life to first make certain nothing from the past will hinder the present journey. For example, the apostle Paul was committed to consistently seeking after the righteousness of Christ. Yet, he recognized that the effectiveness in his present pursuit could be hampered by allowing the past to influence him.

In Philippians 3:12–14 he wrote, *Not that I have already obtained all this, or have already been made perfect, but I press on to take hold of that for which Christ Jesus took hold of me. Brothers, I do not consider myself yet to have taken hold of it. But one thing I do: Forgetting what is behind and straining toward what is ahead, I press on toward the goal to win the prize for which God has called me heavenward in Christ Jesus.* Paul acknowledged that the Christian life is a continual process. Throughout this process, he chose to press on with persistence, knowing that Almighty God who called him would also equip him in every way to accomplish His purposes.

Settle the Past

Even though you've received a call to grow and to become more like Jesus, it can be tempting to get sidetracked by past experiences. To avoid being ineffective in the present, we should ask the Lord to enable us to forget, or settle, what is in the past. Even if the images of past experiences or circumstances are not completely removed from our memory, we should progress to a point where they cease to have a lingering effect, or hold, on us.

For instance, at times the knowledge of past sins can be a detractor from our pursuit of Christ. Rather than dwelling on past sinful behaviors, we have the privilege of asking the Lord for forgiveness; knowing that He will cleanse us from all unrighteousness (1 John 1:9). Since Jesus' forgiveness is complete, we can be free from guilt by seeking His forgiveness (Hebrews 10:19–22). If there are past sins in your life that you haven't asked Christ to forgive, pause now and do so. Then, walk in the freedom true forgiveness brings.

Test and Use Guilt

Sometimes people struggle with feelings of guilt, making it difficult to settle the past. Experiencing a genuine guilty conscience is the result of realizing we've sinned. God uses guilt to convict us, prompting us to change our behavior. In contrast, the enemy uses past behavior to fabricate guilt in an attempt to condemn us.

Since Jesus fully paid our penalty for sin, there is no condemnation for those who believe in Him (Romans 8:1–2). And even though the enemy may accuse us of past sin and the failure to live up to Jesus' righteousness, he lacks the power to convict us. Consequently, his accusations result in false guilt. Be on guard; Satan uses counterfeit guilt to distract us from our true identity and purpose in Christ.

One of the best ways to identify false guilt is to learn to recognize genuine guilt. The Bible tells us that God requires two or three witnesses to establish any issue (2 Corinthians 13:1). This means that He'll use two or three witnesses in the form of His Word and the prompting of His Spirit to point out specific issues in our lives that oppose Him and need correction. The third witness is often the evidence itself of how we've sinned, or "missed the mark," in a particular area of behavior.

While keeping in mind that God uses guilt to establish an issue in our lives for the purpose of urging us toward repentance, read Deuteronomy 19:15: *One witness is not enough to convict a man accused of any crime or offense he may have committed. A matter must be established by the testimony of two or three witnesses.* Did you catch that? One witness isn't enough to convict a person accused of any crime. The enemy is only one witness. The goal of the enemy is not to urge us to repentance, but to distract and disable us with doubts and fears caused by false guilt. While God brings a specific matter to our attention so it can be addressed, Satan attacks with mere accusations that tempt us to remain in a state of guilt rather than experience victory.

It's never God's desire for the guilt of conviction to remain. Dwelling on guilt, when sin has been forgiven, denies the power of God in your life and causes you to focus on self. Instead, you can practice relying on the Holy Spirit to enable you to distinguish true conviction from false accusation, and then embrace only Christ's influence in your life.

Obtain Victory

In addition to dealing with past sinful behaviors and lingering false guilt, at times reminders of prior mistakes, failures, or disappointments can distract us from focusing on the things of God. These types of issues also need to be settled in order to fully pursue Christ's righteousness. Rather than allowing these past experiences to influence your present effectiveness, ask God to show you what He would have you learn from them. Then, pray that the Holy Spirit will help you practice what you've learned. Although as humans we're imperfect, we can ask God to enable us to be victorious in future situations and then press on, trusting Him to do so.

Perhaps you have a past experience of a dramatic or traumatic circumstance that did not involve sin on your part, but it has left undesired memories. These, too, can become a source of distraction in your pursuit of Christ. Scripture teaches that God wants His children to have victory in all things (1 John 5:4–5). Therefore, if you struggle with disquieting memories from your past, begin relying on the Lord's promises to help eliminate any enslaving memories or strongholds. If needed, don't hesitate to seek trustworthy, biblically-based counsel to assist you in this endeavor. Be mindful that complete victory over an experience of this kind may not occur overnight. However, to pursue Christ is to consistently move in the direction of victory.

Press On

Reread Philippians 3:12–14. Because it is difficult to train others to be victorious if you're not living in victory yourself, ask God to help you settle the past and enable you to press on toward the goal of becoming like Jesus. Although there will be times when the enemy tries to use your past against you, it is possible to learn to settle what is behind and to press on day by day, striving to be the living example God has called you to be.

In addition to things past, undesirable or negative, there may be positive experiences in your life that are also a present distraction. Pleasurable experiences can also prevent us from moving in a new direction with Jesus. Although the memories of specific events or seasons of life may be precious to us, we can't live in the past and still move forward with the Lord. Therefore, regardless of the type of former experience, we should develop the habit of letting it go in order to embrace God's current direction.

Are you willing to settle the past so you can fully focus on God's present purpose for your life? Are you willing to let go of past failures, as well as successes, in anticipation of all God desires to accomplish in your future? What practical steps will you take to gain victory over your past?

After settling the past, a believer pursuing righteousness can then begin to intentionally move forward as God directs. Don't misunderstand: a person can make forward strides while working to settle the past. But apart from fully settling past issues, they will experience lingering distractions, limiting personal spiritual victory and effectiveness for Christ's kingdom.

In moving forward, consider this: In much the same way you could use a Global Positioning System to determine both your current location and find help in maneuvering each step of the way to your next destination, God has His system for directing our lives. God provides for us His Word and His Spirit to help us recognize our current spiritual condition and to point us consistently to His will. In order for a GPS to work properly, the receiver must experience limited interference. Similarly, we accurately perceive God's will by receiving His truth when we are free of the world's interference. We can recognize the specific direction God is leading by allowing Him to navigate.

Read Psalm 119:35–37. Notice the Psalmist's invitation for God to navigate his path in life: *Direct me in the path of your commands, for there I find delight. Turn my heart toward your statutes and not toward selfish gain. Turn my eyes away from worthless things; preserve my life according to your word.* Life presents us with many diverse paths to travel on. Although God has a perfect roadmap for each of our lives, He does permit us to choose the paths we take. Understand that the best path for someone else may not be the perfect path for you. Also, you can benefit from examining the paths taken by others in order to learn from their victories and mistakes.

Since each spiritual journey is unique, it's essential to rely on the Lord to discern the specific direction He would have you take. Jeremiah 29:13 tells us, *You will seek me and find me when you seek me with all your heart.* To seek God with wholehearted devotion is to desire His will above all else. Therefore, we're to seek God's will, totally surrendered to His requests and timing. Anything less denies that He knows what is best for us. Sadly, a person who half-heartedly searches for the Lord or runs ahead of His instruction is merely pretending to seek Him while continuing to maintain a sense of personal control. As we abandon our own desires to follow those of Christ, we are truly pursuing His righteousness. So, how can we be certain we're following God's best path?

Invite the Spirit's Heart Assessment

We do this by evaluating our personal walk in light of truth. Psalm 139:23–24 says, *Search me, O God, and know my heart; test me and know my anxious thoughts. See if there is any offensive way in me, and lead me in the way everlasting.* Notice the Psalmist's desire is to be led in the way everlasting, the perfect way of God. In order to follow or align himself with God's will, the Psalmist allowed the Lord to evaluate his spiritual condition by inviting Him to search his heart. Since only God sees the heart of man, He alone can evaluate our heart condition to see whether it is pure and desirous of following His will (Proverbs 21:2).

As we invite the Holy Spirit to bring to mind any "offensive way" or sin against God, we can ask for forgiveness and then change our thought and behavior patterns to reflect obedience to Him. First John 1:9 tells us, *If we confess our sins, he is faithful and just and will forgive us our sins and purify us from all unrighteousness.* Because sin opposes our holy God, unchecked sin in our lives will prevent us from pursuing

His righteousness. Acknowledging personal sin through confession and changing our actions to those that please Jesus testify to His transforming work in our lives.

Just as a disciple desirous of righteous living will allow God to evaluate their heart for sin, their heart should also be examined to determine any impure motives (Proverbs 16:2). It's important to realize that whether or not motives are examined, they are in place prior to action. By inviting the Lord to evaluate our motives, we can then assess if they're pure and pleasing to Him. When we act on motives that are pure, our behavior reflects God's will as we walk in obedience. However, when our motives are less than pure, our actions will be self-seeking, self-promoting, or self-fulfilling. Are you willing to give the Lord an open invitation to examine the condition of your heart? Are you willing to listen and follow what God reveals to you?

As you develop the habit of inviting God to evaluate your heart motives, He will reveal changes that need to take place. Making necessary changes allows you to alter your course of thought and direction to that which pleases God, resulting in obedience.

Motives → Thoughts → Actions → Obedience

Therefore, as you embark on Jesus' call and privilege of discipleship, sincerely ask the Lord to continually purify your heart by aligning your motives, thoughts, and actions with His will. This will help keep you on the path of righteousness.

What means should we use in pursuing righteousness?

Righteousness will never be achieved apart from the work of Jesus Christ; attempting to pursue it by any other means is futile. Consider this: Gasoline is the means by which a car runs properly. If gas isn't used in a car or if some other product is used as a substitute for gas, the car will fail to reach its full potential. The same can be true for our spiritual lives. By design, God has provided us with everything we need for life and godliness through His Word and Spirit (2 Peter 1:3). It's up to us to use the means God has given us to develop a lifestyle of righteousness.

What are potential hazards in pursuing righteousness?

Since it's possible to veer from the path of righteousness, we are to be aware of potential junctures, hazards, and pitfalls that can divert us from an otherwise diligent pursuit. First Peter 5:8–9 says, *Be self-controlled and alert. Your enemy the devil prowls around like a roaring lion looking for someone to devour. Resist him, standing firm in the faith, because you know that your brothers throughout the world are undergoing the same kind of sufferings.*

As you pursue personal holiness, the enemy will not be pleased. Even though he has no authority over you, he will do his best to tempt you to engage in sin, potentially compromising your witness. He will attempt to confuse you and distract you from the things of God. For example, for some people moments of isolation or loneliness create opportunities to turn their focus from the truth of Christ to self. For others, abundance of activity, stress, physical illness, or fatigue cause them to turn inward. Some people are swayed by the temptation to indulge feelings of frustration, anxiety, or disappointment, creating additional spiritual obstacles.

Regardless of the source of temptation, we can be alert to the enemy's schemes and resist his ploys by planting our lives firmly in Jesus and His Word. Do you recognize temptations prior to taking action? If not, begin asking God to show you potential temptations and enable you to stand firm against them.

Since we can only stand firm through reliance on God's power (Isaiah 7:9), being confident or prideful in our own abilities can create a spiritual hazard. Consider 1 Corinthians 10:12: *So, if you think you are standing firm, be careful that you don't fall!* Because our integrity can be lost in a matter of minutes, it's wise to heed this warning and be mindful of the necessity of continual reliance on the Holy Spirit to maintain spiritual stability. In whom or what do you find security? In what specific ways do you see yourself growing in reliance on Christ rather than on your own efforts?

Another potential hazard is the temptation to follow in the footsteps of others who profess belief in Christ, but live according to worldly standards. In Philippians 3:17 Paul wrote, *Join with others in following my example, brothers, and take note of those who live according to the pattern we gave you.* Paul told us to take note of those who truly follow Jesus' example by learning to distinguish lives that genuinely demonstrate Christlikeness from those that do not. Those who exemplify Christ do so through actions rather than merely through words (Matthew 7:21).

Are you able to examine the behaviors of others objectively according to the standard of the Bible? If not, ask God to enable you to distinguish those who merely claim to walk with Christ from those whose actions reflect biblical truth. Then, ask God to enable you to follow only those examples that mirror Him. In doing so, you'll be furthering your pursuit of righteousness.

Regardless of potential pitfalls, God will enable us to walk by faith as we trust in Him. Psalm 37:23–24 provides great promise: *If the LORD delights in a man's way, he makes his steps firm; though he stumble, he will not fall, for the LORD upholds him with his hand.* Jesus delights in our way when we're pursuing Him. As we consistently walk in the path of righteousness, the Lord will cause our steps to be firmly planted there. Although our human weaknesses and imperfections may cause us to stumble in error, at times, His sustaining power will keep us from falling away from truth.

Who and what should we take with us on this journey of righteousness?

In considering those who might join you in pursuing Christ, it's important to know that you can only take someone as far as you've gone yourself. It's not enough to merely talk about the things of the Lord; walking in obedience must be lived out by modeling it for others to follow. This means that we must not only consider holiness to be a personal pursuit, but are to also consider the significant impact our walk with Christ, or lack thereof, could have on others. This isn't to say that we must be perfect before attempting to disciple others. If that were the case, no one would be qualified to do so. However, recognizing that pursing holiness has the potential to influence others to follow Jesus should cause us to further evaluate our lifestyle.

Philippians 1:27 tells us, *Whatever happens, conduct yourselves in a manner worthy of the gospel of Christ.* For the sake of Christ, regardless of the situation or circumstance, God has called us and will enable us to accurately represent His standard of truth for others to follow.

In what specific ways does your life consistently and accurately reflect Christ? Begin today asking the Lord to transform you into an effective ambassador for His kingdom (2 Corinthians 5:19–21).

In addition to being mindful of those we may impact for Christ, we should also be aware of the potential spiritual influence of others in our lives. If you don't already have someone in your life that calls you to account for your actions, prayerfully consider inviting someone to do so. Those you may ask to hold you accountable could be peers or someone older and should be more spiritually mature than you. They should be able to correctly communicate and apply the Word of God, be committed to obeying it, and able to convey truth in love.

Because God knows what is absolutely best for you, those who truly have your best interest in mind will consistently point you to the truth of God's character and His Word. In other words, those who point you to truth, regardless of whether or not it is difficult to say or well received, are those who genuinely have God's best in mind for you. Since disciples are to be above reproach, accountability for personal behavior is essential in pursuing righteousness.

What will this journey cost?

For many people the cost is the determining factor in any endeavor. How does the cost fit into your decision-making process? The apostle Paul counted the cost of pursuing personal holiness and chose to commit his life to faithfully following Jesus. In Philippians 3:7–9 he wrote, *But whatever was to my profit I now consider loss for the sake of Christ. What is more, I consider everything a loss compared to the surpassing greatness of knowing Christ Jesus my Lord, for whose sake I have lost all things. I consider them rubbish, that I may gain Christ and be found in him, not having a righteousness of my own that comes from the law, but that which is through faith in Christ—the righteousness that comes from God and is by faith.*

Paul not only considered all things apart from Christ as loss, but also was willing to lose all things to know Christ more intimately. Paul desired to experience complete dependence on Jesus and genuine righteousness through a growing faith in Him. Are you able to distinguish the eternal benefits of knowing Christ Jesus from the temporal pleasures offered by the world? Is there anything you are unwilling to lose for the sake of following Christ? If so, in what ways could those things possibly be a hindrance to your walk with Jesus?

As you travel this journey in pursuit of holiness, God doesn't promise it will be easy or without cost. But He does promise to be with you every step of the way (Joshua 1:5; Matthew 28:20). Also, the blessings resulting from a consecrated life are immeasurable (Ephesians 3:20–21). In 1 Timothy 4:16, we are encouraged to stay the course of righteousness: *Watch your life and doctrine closely. Persevere in them, because if you do, you will save both yourself and your hearers.* As you persevere in developing personal spiritual disciplines, your life's journey will consistently conform to the likeness of Christ, and those observing will be drawn to Jesus.

CHAPTER FOUR

The Bible: God's Discipleship Manual

Just as there are effective tools used for other forms of work, Scripture is the most effective tool for discipleship training. God's Word reveals how we can obtain everything we will ever need for life and godliness (2 Peter 1:3–4). Even so, it is up to each of us, as individuals, to choose to follow God's manual for living.

Pursue Biblical Truth

Psalm 119:10–16 provides a wonderful example of one who earnestly pursues biblical truth: *I seek you with all my heart; do not let me stray from your commands. I have hidden your word in my heart that I might not sin against you. Praise be to you, O LORD; teach me your decrees. With my lips I recount all the laws that come from your mouth. I rejoice in following your statutes as one rejoices in great riches. I meditate on your precepts and consider your ways. I delight in your decrees; I will not neglect your word.* Notice how practical and diligent the Psalmist is in studying, meditating on, memorizing, and applying God's Word. If we truly desire to please the Lord, we, too, will be sincere in following this example. In what practical ways are you allowing God's Word to permeate your daily life?

The truth is, you won't experience long-term success without a plan. Therefore, make a plan today for the Bible to pervade your life. Rather than setting unrealistic goals for yourself in this area, set goals that are practical, and then be diligent in pursuing them. Ask God to show you opportunities to spend time reading and studying His Word. Then, rather than fill these appointed times with other activities, spend this quality time alone with Him.

If you don't already have a plan to meditate on and memorize Scripture, choose one of the Bible verses that impresses you as you read this book. Write it out and post it in several obvious places to view throughout the day. Meditate on the words and their meaning. Ask the Holy Spirit to supernaturally enable you to remember God's truth. Consider what it would look like for you to apply this specific truth in your life and begin practicing its principles. Then, build from there by consistently applying new verses of Scripture. As you continually put into practice God's principles, your knowledge and understanding of Scripture will increase and God will bless your obedience.

Prepare to Speak Truth

In 2 Timothy 4:2, Paul conveyed this charge to Timothy: *Preach the Word; be prepared in season and out of season; correct, rebuke and encourage—with great patience and careful instruction.* Paul makes it clear that we're to communicate God's Word. The key to being able to share God's Word in any given moment lies in the preparation to do so.

Consider this: While in the midst of their studies, do you think nursing students anticipate one day using what they've learned to help patients with their physical needs? Isn't that the goal of their training? In much the same way, we should anticipate using what God is teaching us to enhance the spiritual well-being of others.

From my personal experience, I regret those moments when an opportunity presented itself to witness to others, and I was unprepared with what to say. I was content with helping to meet their physical needs while often failing to consider my potential role in meeting their spiritual needs. For example, I might provide clothing to the needy, visit the sick in the hospital, or even bake a casserole to minister to a hurting family, but then what? It is important to understand that, while these efforts can be significant, apart from sharing the truth of Jesus, they may fail to make a lasting spiritual impact. When the clothes wear out, the person is dismissed from the hospital, or the casserole is gone, those people will have nothing to support them. While Christ's love expressed through deeds can be compelling, it is His Word that equips and sustains us through the challenging moments of life. Therefore, we should be prepared to patiently and carefully communicate Scripture in any situation.

First Peter 4:11 says, *If anyone speaks, he should do it as one speaking the very words of God. If anyone serves, he should do it with the strength God provides, so that in all things God may be praised through Jesus Christ. To him be the glory and the power for ever and ever. Amen.* Notice that our objective is for God to be praised and glorified in all things. Just imagine the moments of your daily life being continually characterized by praise and glory to Jesus our Lord. Now imagine the influence that way of life could have in the lives of those around you.

Consistently choosing to empty ourselves and allow God's Word and His power to become greater within us, as 1 Peter 4:11 suggests, will take practice. As you daily study God's Word, ask the Holy Spirit to allow the Scripture to become ingrained in you, exchanging any personal ideas or assumptions contrary to truth for godly principles. Then, throughout the day practice considering whether or not the information you're communicating can be linked to biblical truth. If not, then the information may reflect personal opinion or theory.

Ask God to show you those times when you begin communication with such phrases as "I feel," "If you want my opinion," or "If it were me." Then, ask the Holy Spirit to help you recognize the opportunity to communicate truth and enable you to recall pertinent Scripture. Practice removing any personal influence you may have in the conversation by pointing to God's principles. This can be achieved by choosing to precede statements with phrases such as "God's Word tells us," or "According to Scripture."

Hebrews 4:12 says, *For the word of God is living and active. Sharper than any double-edged sword, it penetrates even to dividing soul and spirit, joints and marrow; it judges the thoughts and attitudes of the heart.* Only God's Word is powerful enough to penetrate a person's inner self, where genuine change begins. The Bible alone is capable of convicting one's heart and prompting one to change undesired behavior. Therefore, we are to use the Word of God as often as possible rather than our own words.

The habit of exchanging personal thoughts and opinions for the absolute truth of Scripture and using it in exchange for your own words will consistently point others to Jesus. As you persist in practicing these principles, the Holy Spirit will enable you to develop them into a lifestyle. In doing so, others will see Christ at work in you and He will be honored.

When presenting truth to others, God wants us to focus on His Spirit and His Word rather than be concerned about our personal style and delivery. In 1 Corinthians 2:1–5, Paul was writing to the church at Corinth: *When I came to you, brothers, I did not come with eloquence or superior wisdom as I proclaimed to you the testimony about God. For I resolved to know nothing while I was with you except Jesus Christ and him crucified. I came to you in weakness and fear, and with much trembling. My message and my preaching were not with wise and persuasive words, but with a demonstration of the Spirit's power, so that your faith might not rest on men's wisdom, but on God's power.*

It is encouraging that even the apostle Paul was aware of his weaknesses, yet even his sense of fear and inadequacy didn't deter him from obedience to his Savior. Paul served from a position of humility and placed his faith in God's power rather than in human wisdom. Since we can't afford to let the faith of others depend on our wisdom, our teaching is to resemble that of the apostle Paul—based on the truth of Jesus and communicated by the Spirit's power.

Trust in the Power of Truth

As we've seen, God uses His Word to convict a person's conscience of the need for repentance. Therefore, we should fully rely on the power of Scripture to convict. In 2 Corinthians 4:2, Paul explained the actions of Jesus' followers: *We have renounced secret and shameful ways; we do not use deception, nor do we distort the word of God. On the contrary, by setting forth the truth plainly we commend ourselves to every man's conscience in the sight of God.* We are to follow this example today by plainly speaking truth, carefully presenting it with clarity.

As we strive to convey God's Word correctly under His authority, we can trust that He will use it for His glory. Isaiah 55:10–11 confirms this promise: *As the rain and the snow come down from heaven, and do not return to it without watering the earth and making it bud and flourish, so that it yields seed for the sower and bread for the eater, so is my word that goes out from my mouth: It will not return to me empty, but will accomplish what I desire and achieve the purpose for which I sent it.*

In the same way that we can't always see the immediate effects of moisture on developing plants, we may not see the immediate effects of God's Word taking root in the hearts of those we are trying to influence. Regardless of whether we witness immediate spiritual fruit, we can trust the truth that was communicated in His power to fulfill its intended purpose. Do you have full trust in the power of God's Word to affect change in the lives of others?

Include All God's Commands

As we further consider the significance of using God's Word in making disciples, let's once again remind ourselves of Matthew 28:19–20: *"Therefore go and make disciples of all nations, baptizing them in the name of the Father and of the Son and of the Holy Spirit, and teaching them to obey everything I have commanded you.* By using the word "everything" here, Jesus is all-inclusive concerning His instructions; nothing is to be overlooked when teaching His commands. In addition, God's commands are to be fully obeyed. Just as Jesus fully obeyed the directives of God the Father, we, too, are to become examples of Jesus by obeying all God's commands.

In order for others to fully obey God's instructions, His commands must be communicated and understood in their correct context. Deuteronomy 4:2 says, *Do not add to what I command you and do not subtract from it, but keep the commands of the LORD your God that I give you.* Be careful: God doesn't need us to enhance His Word, nor does He want us to omit instructions that may be difficult to say or receive.

Some groups and organizations, even those considered Christian, have taken unnecessary liberties through dramatic portrayals of Scripture. In addition, individuals have chosen to speculate on subject matter that isn't directly covered in the Bible, or have elaborated on God's Word in the hope of making it more culturally relevant. Jesus calls His disciples to be prudent in such matters. If we try to enhance Scripture, we risk misinterpreting truth and, thereby, potentially endangering the spiritual well-being of others. If we subtract things from God's complete Word, we may delay or hinder a person's spiritual progress.

In some instances, Scripture may need to be simplified or clarified for better understanding, but never changed. Also, we're to be vigilant in communicating Scripture in its correct context (2 Timothy 2:15). This doesn't mean that we'll always have all the correct answers, but that we are responsible to use God's Word correctly when speaking into the lives of others. On those occasions when you're uncertain of a correct answer, let others know that further research or counsel is needed to answer the question. Then, research and reply to their questions as soon as possible.

Develop Critical Thinking Skills

Titus 2:11–12 tells us, *For the grace of God that brings salvation has appeared to all men. It teaches us to say "No" to ungodliness and worldly passions, and to live self-controlled, upright and godly lives in this present age.* Our loving God provided His standard of living so we can more easily discern the lies presented by the world and distinguish godly behavior from worldly passions.

Jesus wants us to be alert to the world's influences that oppose truth and lead some to believe that sinful behavior is driven by a given circumstance. Others may view closely following God's commands as legalistic and a disregard of His grace and mercy. Through the consistent practice of using Scripture to distinguish godliness from worldly passions, we can each develop a lifestyle that accurately determines God's will (Romans 12:2). In order to use Scripture effectively, we must first be able to think critically.

Sometimes people are led to believe that thinking critically makes them critical of themselves or others. However, this is not true. Being critical is finding fault or pointing out error. Thinking critically merely helps us arrive at the best answer by objectively examining issues and circumstances, while considering possible choices and consequences. For example, if we needed to cross a busy street, we would use critical thinking skills to objectively evaluate the traffic flow, available crosswalks, and traffic signals to determine the best time and means to cross safely.

Critical thinking improves one's problem-solving skills, making it particularly beneficial in the life of a Christ-follower. As we learn to think critically, using the standard of truth set forth in the Bible, our thoughts will no longer be conformed to those of the world. Instead, our thoughts will be based on absolute truth and, therefore, will be useful for effectively determining God's will. Are you in the habit of using Scripture to find God's will? How have you recently used God's Word to help you make a decision? In what situation have you applied a biblical principle to support a decision?

Before training someone else to develop critical thinking skills, it will be valuable for you to first hone your own by learning to ask Christ-centered questions. Then you can use this method effectively with others. In doing so, you'll be teaching each person to ask themselves Christ-centered questions. Asking questions that reflect truth can help a person recognize thoughts and actions that echo the world's view and those that mirror biblical truth.

Also, it's important to help each person arrive at the correct answer for themselves, instead of pointing them directly to the best solution. This will assist them in becoming spiritually self-disciplined. Since it's likely that a person will not choose to change a behavior unless they first recognize it, answers to spiritually driven questions can hold great significance.

A person who has not experienced this method of training may not initially appreciate it. However, we can see the benefits of using questions by studying the following examples from Scripture. After Adam and Eve sinned in the Garden of Eden, the Bible tells us that they hid from the Lord. In Genesis 3:9, God called to Adam, "Where are you?" We understand that God is all-knowing and, therefore, very aware of Adam and Eve's physical location. God used this question and those that followed to prompt Adam and Eve to consider their spiritual condition.

The Lord also used questions to lead Cain in thinking about his spiritual well-being. Genesis 4:6–9 tells us, *Then the LORD said to Cain, "Why are you angry? Why is your face downcast? If you do what is right, will you not be accepted? But if you do not do what is right, sin is crouching at your door; it desires to have you, but you must master it."*

Now Cain said to his brother Abel, "Let's go out to the field." And while they were in the field, Cain attacked his brother Abel and killed him.

Then the LORD said to Cain, "Where is your brother Abel?"

Notice how these questions could have prompted Cain to consider impure motive, the choice between right and wrong, the benefits of obedience, and the consequence of sin. Further questioning provided a means for Cain to acknowledge his sin and to recognize the opportunity to seek forgiveness. How tragic that Cain failed to take God's questions to heart. If he had done so, his choices and actions may have been much different.

In Matthew 16:13–15, Jesus asked some key questions of His followers: *When Jesus came to the region of Caesarea Philippi, he asked his disciples, "Who do people say the Son of Man is?"*

They replied, "Some say John the Baptist; others say Elijah; and still others, Jeremiah or one of the prophets."

"But what about you?" he asked. "Who do you say I am?" Jesus wasn't asking these questions because He was experiencing a personal identity crisis. He did so to encourage His disciples to distinguish the truth of His identity from mere theories and popular opinions.

Although this method of training will be more thoroughly covered later in this book, begin now to practice asking questions rather than instantly providing answers. For example: Does God's Word have anything to say about this particular subject? In what ways does this situation reflect the character of God? By asking questions, you're training yourself and others to consider God's perspective.

Use Life Application

In the same way asking questions can encourage others to consider personal application of truth, using relevant life examples from the Bible can also be beneficial in discipleship training. For instance, although Samson had physical strength, he allowed his weaknesses to adversely influence his choices (Judges 13:1 to 16:31). Even though Rahab didn't always have a reputation for godly living, she honored God through her obedience to Him (Joshua 2:1–24). The same prideful Peter who proclaimed he would never disown Jesus (Matthew 26:33–35), did so—not once but three times. He then wept with sincere remorse (Matthew 26:69–75).

Much can be learned from these examples. Even though these lives reveal behavior that displeased God, He used these people in mighty ways when they chose to walk in obedience to His will. Bear in mind that a person can learn as much from someone who does wrong as from someone who does right. Also, lessons learned from knowledge, rather than from poor personal choices, usually result in more favorable consequences. Therefore, it can be valuable to glean knowledge from the lives of Bible characters.

At times, it can be beneficial to provide word pictures or analogies to help others grasp truth as it applies to their situation. For example, in James 3:3–8, both analogies and word pictures are used to help readers understand the human tongue's ability to direct the entire body and the need for the tongue to be brought under control. Through these illustrations, each reader is prompted to consider their personal choice to allow the Holy Spirit to have control over their tongue.

In order for an analogy to have a spiritual impact on its hearers, it should be provided by the Holy Spirit rather than created by man. Consistently rely on the Holy Spirit to give you the words to say and the enablement to link them to the biblical principle being presented. By keeping in mind the ultimate goal for discipleship, teaching others to obey all that God commands, analogies can be helpful tools when learning to follow in obedience.

In training others to conform to Christlike behavior, we may use analogies that will assist people in seeing personal behavior objectively. For example, although King David revered God, he entered into an adulterous relationship with Bathsheba. During this time, David lived in a continuous state of unrepentant sin that included the murder of Bathsheba's husband (2 Samuel 11:1–27). In 2 Samuel 12:1–4, God sent the prophet Nathan to assist David in recognizing the error of his ways. Nathan did so through the use of an applicable analogy.

Notice that Nathan's words and guidance were from the Lord: *The LORD sent Nathan to David. When he came to him, he said, "There were two men in a certain town, one rich and the other poor. The rich man had a very large number of sheep and cattle, but the poor man had nothing except one little ewe lamb he had bought. He raised it, and it grew up with him and his children. It shared his food, drank from his cup and even slept in his arms. It was like a daughter to him.*

Now a traveler came to the rich man, but the rich man refrained from taking one of his own sheep or cattle to prepare a meal for the traveler who had come to him. Instead, he took the ewe lamb that belonged to the poor man and prepared it for the one who had come to him."

Second Samuel 12:5–6 reveals that David clearly understood the wrongdoing of the man in the story. Then in verse 7, Nathan linked the behavior of the man to David's actions by saying, "*You are the man!*" In verse 13, David acknowledged his sin before God and repentance followed. Even so, the consequences of sin remained. God used His servant Nathan by equipping him with a purposeful analogy to assist in David's repentance and restoration. As with Nathan, God will equip us today to effectively guide others to truth. In what ways are you relying on God to give you the words He desires others to have, rather than giving them those you would choose?

Regardless of the uniqueness of an individual or their spiritual journey, God's standard for living is one-size-fits-all. God's Word is perfect, unchanging, infallible, and applicable for all things—making it the perfect instruction manual for discipleship training.

CHAPTER FIVE

The Significance of Abiding

As we further consider personal discipleship and the influence our lives could have in discipling others, the significance of a very intimate, abiding relationship with Jesus becomes apparent. To abide in Christ is to dwell with Him, to avail ourselves of His presence, to continually be connected to, or "plugged in" to His power; depending on Him for all things. Do these words describe your relationship with our precious Lord?

When we fail to abide in Christ, there is a disconnect from the Holy Spirit that affects our thinking, discernment, decision making, and behavior. For this reason, as we navigate each day, we're to consistently commune with Him. Jesus described an abiding relationship with Him in John 15:5: *"I am the vine; you are the branches. If a man remains in me and I in him, he will bear much fruit, apart from me you can do nothing.*" In this verse, Jesus provides a word picture referring to Himself as the vine and His followers as the branches.

A branch receives everything needed to sustain life from the vine and cannot survive without it. In the same way that a branch must stay attached to the vine to accomplish its purpose, we, too, must stay connected to Jesus to accomplish His purpose for us. The purpose of a branch is to bear the physical fruit that resembles the type of plant it grows from. Similarly, God's purpose for believers is to bear spiritual fruit that reflects Jesus, the One we live for.

Some people find it difficult to understand how their efforts will fail apart from Christ's involvement. After all, consider the mass fame and fortune that has been achieved through the efforts of man. It's true that apart from Christ individuals as well as groups may accomplish much. However, Jesus made it known that those achievements have no eternal value.

If it's truly your desire to influence others for His kingdom, it's vital that you abide in Jesus, consistently delighting in His presence while inviting Him to speak into your life through His Word. As a result, you'll experience an increased awareness of His leading and guidance in the details and decisions made throughout your daily life. But there is still a choice to be made—the choice of whether to rely on Christ to help you walk in obedience.

Let's think about it. We can choose to guess or presume we have the correct answers, or we can choose to trust the wisdom of our all-knowing God. We can choose to rely on God's leading or base our decisions on circumstances or feelings. We can depend on God's unlimited strength or on our own limited abilities: the choice is ours. When we disconnect from Christ, we are choosing to have our own way—operating apart from Him. By remaining connected to Christ, attached to the vine, we have every means available to experience victory in any situation.

In addition to experiencing victory, walking in obedience to the authority of Christ Jesus results in freedom. Do you desire to experience the victory and freedom that result from abiding in Christ? Are you willing to take practical steps to learn to tap into and remain connected to God's supernatural resources?

A lifestyle of abiding in Jesus begins by developing a mind set on pursuing His will (Romans 12:2; Colossians 3:1–2). This means that you decide to lay down your own desires in order to seek His, to give up selfish ways for God's perfect way and let go of your own agenda in pursuit of God's perfect plan. In doing so, you're preparing your heart and mind not only to hear what God has to say but also to receive what is said. The next step is to follow through by becoming more intimate with God through personal conversation and reliance on Him.

Abiding through Prayer

The apostle Paul understood that communication was vital to having an intimate relationship with Jesus and instructed us specifically in 1 Thessalonians 5:17: *Pray continually.* The word prayer merely refers to the way we speak with God. As with other relationships, good communication develops as a result of both talking and listening. Since God already knows what is on our hearts and minds, we should be at ease sharing our thoughts and concerns with Him. As we learn to listen to God, we'll become sensitive to the prompting of His Spirit and enabled to receive His wisdom and guidance.

Some people may find it objectionable to take every matter of their lives to the Lord in prayer. After all, God created us with a mind so we could think for ourselves. However, it's the very act of thinking for ourselves that influences us to follow selfish desires rather than the ways of God. Can you relate?

Proverbs 16:2 states, *All a man's ways seem innocent to him, but motives are weighed by the LORD.* Apart from inviting the Lord to examine or to weigh our motives, how can we be assured that they're pure and pleasing to Him? Proverbs 21:2 concurs, *All a man's ways seem right to him, but the LORD weighs the heart.* There will be times when our thoughts, plans, and actions feel right to us, yet do not represent God's best. For this reason, we should consistently invite the Holy Spirit to evaluate our desires, motives, and behavior, and allow Him to make any necessary corrections. As we grow in an intimate relationship with Jesus, we'll become increasingly discerning of His will. Is it your habit to invite the Holy Spirit to check and correct your motives and desires?

To be successful in abiding in Christ, it's beneficial to formulate a daily plan. Psalm 5:3 says, *In the morning, O LORD, you hear my voice; in the morning I lay my requests before you and wait in expectation.* As the Psalmist did, begin each day with the Lord. Before your feet hit the floor, acknowledge each day as a gift from God and thank Him for it. This will assist you in centering your immediate focus on Christ. Although you may have a daily routine and thoughts of what may occur during the day, commit your schedule to God's care, trusting that His plans are best. Invite God to evaluate your motives and ask Him to enable you to be flexible, open, and available to what He desires to accomplish through you. Communicate with the Lord, sharing openly those thoughts and concerns that are on your heart and mind.

Then, anticipate Him working on your behalf. Further, develop a habit of abiding in Jesus throughout each day by continually communicating your thoughts and concerns to Him, and by relying on Him to respond to your personal needs. As a result, you'll be thoroughly equipped to handle any situation, and God will receive the glory. Are you ready to relinquish each moment of your life to the leading and guidance of Christ Jesus?

Psalm 63:6 tells us, *On my bed, I remember you [God]; I think of you through the watches of the night.* Even through sleepless hours of the night, the Psalmist chose to stay connected to the Lord, viewing these wakeful moments as opportunities to pray and abide in Him. When God allows you to be awakened, practice asking Him to show you anything He would like you to know. Then, commit those things to the Lord.

In Colossians 4:2 Paul wrote, *Devote yourselves to prayer, being watchful and thankful.* Paul is instructing us to dedicate ourselves to prayer by developing a lifestyle of diligence in personal communication with God. Persisting in prayer enables us to be continually focused on Christ while developing intimacy in worship. In addition, being disciplined in listening to the Lord allows God to reveal His will to our hearts and minds. Just as Paul was watchful and thankful, we, too, should have grateful hearts as we anticipate God working on our behalf.

Notice in Colossians 4:3 Paul's desire to follow God's will rather than lead in his own way: *And pray for us, too, that God may open a door for our message, so that we may proclaim the mystery of Christ, for which I am in chains.* Since no one comes to Christ apart from God drawing them (John 6:44), we should become increasingly sensitive to open doors of opportunity that Christ provides for sharing His truth with others. Consistent communication with God allows Him opportunity to reveal appointments to us, freeing us from the temptation to create work for ourselves. Because the work is His, a genuine disciple will seek God's will through prayer and then follow where He leads.

Let's take a moment to review Matthew 28:19-20 to help us further understand the role abiding plays in fulfilling the Great Commission: *"Go and make disciples of all nations, baptizing them in the name of the Father and of the Son and of the Holy Spirit, and teaching them to obey everything I have commanded you."*

Lost ··· Salvation ··· Baptism ··· Obedience to all God Commands →

The initial part of our commission is to make disciples of all nations, which comes before the instruction to baptize. Because salvation occurs prior to baptism, we know that Jesus wants us to first and foremost share the gospel of His grace. We are then to baptize those who believe the gospel, followed by teaching them to obey everything Jesus commanded. This means that, as we set out to make disciples, the people we encounter could possibly be at many different places in their spiritual journey.

In order for us to be effective in the lives of others, Jesus must reveal to us a person's spiritual needs. If we mistakenly act on assumptions, we could provide information beyond what someone needs or can comprehend, expect too little or too much from them, or possibly offend. Therefore, we should depend deeply on the Holy Spirit for wisdom and guidance. Again, we can see the importance of choosing to continually abide in the Lord. Without abiding, the necessary discernment will not be ours.

Abiding in God's Word and Power

In addition to prayer, abiding in Christ through His Word and power prepares us to effectively convey truth in any given moment. In 1 Corinthians 3:6–7 Paul wrote, *I planted the seed, Apollos watered it, but God made it grow. So neither he who plants nor he who waters is anything, but only God, who makes things grow.* There may be times when God directs you to plant seed by conveying truth to someone for the first time. On other occasions, perhaps you'll water it by building on truth previously shared by others. Keep in mind that apart from the truth of Jesus, we have nothing of any eternal value to offer anyone. Rather than giving a person what you may want them to receive, provide each person with what God knows they need, as He reveals it to you. In doing so, you'll be operating under Christ's authority to achieve His purpose.

Prior to commissioning His disciples for service, Jesus reminded them of the authority by which they would be sent (Matthew 28:18–19). Jesus was not just expressing the authority given to Him by God the Father. He also wanted His disciples to understand that He was sending them out under this same authority. As we begin the process of preparing to train others in discipleship, it can sometimes be challenging to determine our specific obligations in this area of service. As we abide in Jesus, we seek to do nothing on our own but consistently remain under His authority. By walking under God's authority and control, we can rely fully on Him to show us what to do and what to refrain from doing in each situation. Then, if we are tempted to doubt or fear, we can know and trust that we are operating in Christ's strength rather than in our own.

CHAPTER SIX

Recognizing Opportunities

As we grow in personal discipleship, we should be consistently preparing to influence others for Christ's kingdom and be anticipating opportunities to do so. Anticipating occasions to influence others for Jesus is similar to anticipating other opportunities in life. For example, when you get behind the wheel of your car, you are preparing to drive. In operating within the rules of the road, you anticipate opportunities to move forward, stop, yield, and turn as directed. Similarly, when you abide in Jesus, you are preparing and anticipating opportunities to represent Him to others. As you follow Christ's lead, He will guide your path.

In addition to anticipating divine opportunities, it's important that we are also prepared to recognize them. The Bible teaches that God is always working around us (John 5:17) and has purpose in all things (Romans 8:28). As a result, every moment has the potential to be a teachable moment. Did you catch that? It's possible that the God of the universe has something to reveal about Himself, to us or to others around us, each moment of every day! Knowing this should motivate us to become consistently aware of opportunities and intentional about conveying truth throughout each day.

In John 15:16 Jesus said, "*You did not choose me, but I chose you and appointed you to go and bear fruit—fruit that will last. Then the Father will give you whatever you ask in my name.*" It is amazing that Almighty God desires to include us in His work and has appointed to each of us opportunities to bear fruit for His kingdom. Remember, the only fruit that will last is that which is produced from the eternal things of God rather than the temporal things of this world. As you begin to invest eternally in the lives of others, God will enable you to produce eternal fruit.

While developing a heart for discipleship and a desire to invest truth in the lives of others, the limitations of being just one person can sometimes be overwhelming. Because we can never be in two places at one time, it's important to gain clear understanding of the specific work God has appointed each of us to do. God is perfect and has a perfect and purposeful plan for our lives (Jeremiah 29:11). Therefore, a wise person will pursue God's plan, looking for His purpose in each situation rather than relying on personal understanding or preference. God's orchestrated opportunities may not always be obvious or convenient. They may not produce the results we may expect or desire; but, they are always purposeful.

What influences you to commit to an activity or appointment? In what ways does God confirm His will and direction in your life? Rather than assume what God might want you to accomplish in any given moment, practice relying on the Spirit's prompting and provision to achieve His will.

As we pursue God's will in all we do, He will reveal His best path or direction for our lives (Proverbs 3:5–6). If we choose to do things God does not ask of us, then we risk performing tasks in our own strength and may miss an opportunity that He did create for us. Also, in operating outside of God's will, we potentially place ourselves outside His protection and, therefore, cannot expect His blessing. Instead of trying to influence others on our own, we are to allow the Lord to consistently guide us and do the work through us. As a result, God will receive honor and glory as His will is accomplished.

Ephesians 2:10 tells us, *For we are God's workmanship, created in Christ Jesus to do good works, which God prepared in advance for us to do.* God's desire for each of His disciples is to bring Him glory, so He prepares both the work and the heart of each worker to reflect His character and truth. Before the beginning of time, Creator God designed specific work for each of us to do. It's our job to develop the habit of asking God to enable us to distinguish the work He is calling us to, from that which He is not. Then, we are to trust fully in Him by following His lead.

For example, a young adult senses God's call to commit to serve in the youth department where he attends church. At the same church, the preschool department has a larger number of children in attendance and greater leadership needs. However (and this is a big "however"), the young adult is not called by God to serve in the preschool department. (Because disciples of Jesus follow His lead, not the lead of others, service is to be based on God's call without substitution.) Therefore, in order to walk in obedience to Christ, the young adult should trust God's leading to serve in the youth department.

In another example, you receive two invitations to attend weddings on the same date. Due to logistics, you can't attend both. Your choice can either be based on such things as convenience, the closeness of your relationship to the couple, or the expectations of others. Or, you can acknowledge God having purpose in every circumstance by seeking His will. Also, it is wise to realize that God may lead you to attend one wedding or the other, or He may show you to abstain from both. By following God's lead, you can be where He asks you to be while trusting Him to fulfill His purpose. Living this way can be freeing as well as a testimony to others that God is directing your life.

Relying on God's discernment for our lives takes the guesswork out of where we should go and what we should be doing. This will take practice and discipline. For example, rather than responding to a request based on an opening in your schedule, establish the habit of asking the Lord to show you how to best fill that time. Instead of automatically making decisions, practice asking Him for direction. For instance, rather than immediately taking a seat at church, ask the Holy Spirit to guide you into His plan and purpose. Perhaps He will direct you to someone who needs to feel welcome, a kind touch, or a word of encouragement. Although we will study this point more in future chapters, stop now to consider the potential difference it would make if we viewed each moment of our lives as an invitation to fulfill a specific purpose. Then ask the Lord to enable you to recognize His appointed opportunities throughout each day.

In Acts 16:6–10, Paul's sensitivity to the discernment of the Holy Spirit concerning specific appointments is evident: *Paul and his companions traveled throughout the region of Phyrgia and Galatia, having been kept by the Holy Spirit from preaching the word in the province of Asia. When they came to the border of Mysia, they tried to enter Bithynia, but the Spirit of Jesus would not allow them to. So they passed by Mysia and went down to Troas. During the night Paul had a vision of a man of Macedonia standing and begging him, "Come over to Macedonia and help us." After Paul had seen the vision, we got ready at once to leave for Macedonia, concluding that God had called us to preach the gospel to them.* Paul is an excellent example of a life fully dependent on the leading and guidance of the Holy Spirit. He didn't question the Lord or convey his opinion concerning who might benefit most from his ministry, nor did he ask for the easiest way. Instead he willingly embraced God's plan.

As you encounter people throughout each day, ask God to show you His will in each specific instance. Be open and sensitive to the leading of the Holy Spirit, trusting Him to give you wisdom and direction. Just as He did for Paul, God will reveal to you what He is and is not calling you to do. Although others may not always understand or agree with the choices you make, relying on God's direction allows you to point them to Him in defense of your decisions. As you anticipate God's leading, you can follow through with confidence, doing those works He has appointed for you.

CHAPTER SEVEN

Being Intentionally Relational

Now that we've learned to anticipate and recognize the work God has prepared for us, we'll look at ways to act on these open doors of divine opportunity. Knowing that God's ultimate goal is for us to reproduce His truth in the lives of others, it makes sense that opportunities for His kingdom's service will involve people. For this reason, we should learn to relate effectively to the people God places in our lives.

God loves us so very much that He sent Jesus to earth as the means by which we can enter into a relationship with Him. As Christ-followers, it should be our life's endeavor to help others recognize the eternal relationship with God that is available through Jesus. In order to do so, we must love others and learn to relate to them as Jesus did.

Throughout His life, Jesus continually related to those around Him. However, Jesus chose to be relational with purpose—the significant purpose of sharing truth. We see this in John chapter 4. As Jesus was traveling through Samaria, He stopped to rest at Jacob's well. Verses 7, 9–10 record, *When a Samaritan woman came to draw water, Jesus said to her, "Will you give me a drink?"*

The Samaritan woman said to him, "You are a Jew and I am a Samaritan woman. How can you ask me for a drink?" (For Jews do not associate with Samaritans.)

Jesus answered her, "If you knew the gift of God and who it is that asks you for a drink, you would have asked him and he would have given you living water." He took the subject of water and immediately related it to eternal truth. In doing so, the woman's personal need for truth was revealed. Jesus continued to use truth in their dialogue, cultivating change in the heart and life of this woman.

First Thessalonians 2:13 clearly shows how truth can be effective in the life of an individual: *And we also thank God continually because, when you <u>received</u> the word of God, which you <u>heard</u> from us, you <u>accepted</u> it not as the word of men, but as it actually is, the word of God, which is at work in you who <u>believe</u>.* (Emphasis added.) Because genuine change occurs within the heart, the truth of God's Word must be internalized before it can affect a person's life. In other words, for Scripture to create change within a life, it must be received as valuable and then trusted as it is applied to living. Then, as the person depends on Christ, He will enable them to live out biblical truth. That is why our ability to relate well to others can be instrumental in the personal development of a relationship with Christ. Is it your goal to cultivate relationships for the purpose of sharing the truth of Jesus or merely to build friendships?

Jesus was very intentional with His relationships. He met people where they were and spoke in ways they could best understand truth. This is a significant point to realize: Sharing biblical truth is what sets us apart from the world! Many groups create ways to socialize and network with people, using various arenas to bond and build relationships. Although these functions may serve a purpose, a disciple's ultimate goal should be to share the truth of Jesus, and the truth of Jesus is what makes a relationship meaningful. Jesus saw purpose in every conversation, every meeting, and every relationship!

This lifestyle of intentionally cultivating relationships for the purpose of sharing truth may appear to be all consuming. In fact, I have been asked the question, "Does everything always have to be about Jesus?" As I prayerfully considered a response to this query, God provided a question in return, "What portion of our lives should be independent of Him?"

Prior to providing what believers refer to as the Great Commission, Jesus instructed us to follow the Greatest Commandment in Matthew 22:37–38: "*'Love the Lord your God with all your heart and with all your soul and with all your mind.' This is the first and greatest commandment.*" Because we convey to God our love through obedience (1 John 5:3), He desires this commandment to have priority in the lives of His disciples. In order to love God with your entire being, which is humanly impossible, you must first be consumed by Him. This happens as you allow God's Word and the influence of His Spirit to penetrate your heart and mind. As a result, you can then serve Christ with wholehearted devotion.

Take a moment to consider the difference it would make if you chose to love God with your entire being: your individual characteristics, your physical and emotional qualities, your will, your thoughts, and your decision-making processes. In what specific ways does your life reflect the greatest commandment? As we strive to make disciples of others, may God consume each of us with His truth, unconditional love, and desire to see people come to know Him! Study the remainder of this chapter while considering ways you can intentionally convey Christ's love when relating to others.

Focus on Jesus

Our words and actions are a product of our inner self. If we are sincere in building relationships for the purpose of conveying truth, then our hearts and minds will be focused on the source of truth— Jesus Christ. If our focus is not on Christ, it will naturally be on someone or something else. As a result, our conversations may point to ourselves, other people, or things rather than the truth of Jesus.

If our focus is on Christ and relating His truth to those around us, we will view them as God does and set aside our own desires. We will meet others where they are rather than expect them to meet us where we are. In other words, rather than ask someone to relate to us, we will strive to be Christlike by choosing to relate to them. The apostle Paul demonstrated this by setting aside his personal desires, social status, and pride to win others to Jesus, all without compromising truth (1 Corinthians 9:19–23).

Consider Your Audience

To relate to others effectively for God's kingdom, we should be mindful, as Paul was, of our audience. For example, I sometimes join friends in volunteering at a local homeless shelter. Our duties usually include distributing food and clothing to those in need. But that's not our purpose. Our purpose is to relate to the people around us with the intention of sharing the truth of Jesus. With our potential audience in mind, we consider how to best affect them for Christ. For instance, we're careful about how we present ourselves. We wouldn't want to wear clothing or jewelry that would cause us to stand out from them. Doing so might cause the residents to think that we cannot relate to their circumstances.

Since our goal is to reflect Jesus, rather than draw attention to ourselves, we would also want to carefully consider the topics we choose for conversation. In this case, discussing our families, jobs, or home life may create a sense that we're unable to understand their life situation or incapable of identifying with their needs. As you set out to make disciples, prayerfully consider your potential audience by asking God to lead you in ways that best relate to others.

A person who is effective in being relational has learned to put the importance of people ahead of their own interests. Philippians 2:3 instructs us, *Do nothing out of selfish ambition or vain conceit, but in humility consider others better than yourselves.* As our Lord so graciously set the example for us to follow, we are to humbly place the spiritual well-being of others ahead of any selfish ambition, thereby becoming a servant of Christ (Philippians 2:4–7). For example, rather than dominating a conversation, we should be engaging others and allowing them to talk about their interests. Showing genuine interest in others will help convey their importance to us.

Convey Truth

At the same time, we should be purposeful by consistently sharing truth. Rather than merely relating spiritual principles as they apply to your life, ask the Holy Spirit to give you insight in sharing those things that will be most beneficial to others. Remember, Jesus used the life experiences of others to teach them truth. Through reliance on the Holy Spirit, we can do the same.

By maintaining focus on Christ and His Word, we can quickly move past the things that we don't have in common with others to the unity that Jesus can bring to every relationship. Some people hesitate to approach individuals due to their apparent status or prestige, while other people fail to associate with those who appear unkempt or are treated as outcasts. God is no respecter of persons, and He does not show favoritism (Romans 2:11). Jesus loves others every bit as much as He loves you and me, and He desires to make disciples of all men and women from all walks of life. First Samuel 16:7 says, *"The LORD does not look at the things man looks at. Man looks at the outward appearance, but the LORD looks at the heart."* If it's difficult for you to love others unconditionally, ask the Holy Spirit to enable you to look past outward appearances to see others the way Jesus does.

On a daily basis, God creates a variety of avenues of opportunity for His followers to influence people for His kingdom. As we further examine these occasions of opportunity, we'll also consider the people we may encounter and the ways we can effectively relate to them. For example, there will be many, many people that we pass by or encounter briefly in our lifetime without ever seeing them again. Even though these brief moments may not afford us the opportunity to present the gospel, these are valuable occasions to reflect the character of Jesus or to prompt others to think about Him.

Galatians 5:22 teaches us that the fruit of the Spirit is love, joy, peace, patience, kindness, goodness, faithfulness, gentleness, and self-control. As we allow the Holy Spirit to work in us and through us, the fruit produced, evidenced by our actions, will reveal Christ's nature to others. Reread Galatians 5:22. Stop to ask yourself the following questions to consider what your life may be communicating to those around you.

- In what ways do your actions reveal Jesus' unconditional love for others?
- Would people say your demeanor consistently exudes the joy of the Lord?
- How does your life reflect the peace of Christ?
- Does your body language and tone of voice convey genuine patience?
- Are you kind to everyone? How are you intentionally mirroring God's goodness?
- In what ways do your attitude, words, and actions reflect Christ's faithfulness in your life?
- Would others define your behavior as being harsh or gentle?
- How are you striving to bring your life under the complete control of the Holy Spirit?

Even the simplest actions or deeds throughout our day can allow others to experience the character of Christ. Therefore, even though these questions may seem challenging, they can also be beneficial in evaluating our potential for spiritual effectiveness in the lives of others. Actions such as holding the door open for someone to go ahead of you or conveying a warm smile and friendly greeting reflect the love, patience, and kindness of Jesus. Remember, as Christ's ambassadors, we are called to serve as representatives of Jesus Christ and His kingdom (2 Corinthians 5:20). Whether or not we accurately represent Jesus can have eternal significance for others.

Just as God desires for us to influence others with our actions, He also desires for us to do so with our words. Ephesians 4:29 tells us, *Do not let any unwholesome talk come out of your mouths, but only what is helpful for building others up according to their needs, that it may benefit those who listen.* Also, Ephesians 5:3–4 says, *But among you there must not be even a hint of sexual immorality, or of any kind of impurity, or of greed, because these are improper for God's holy people. Nor should there be obscenity, foolish talk or coarse joking, which are out of place, but rather thanksgiving.*

In representing Christ, it's beneficial to realize that even the smallest trace of impurity can taint our thoughts, conversations, and actions, resulting in misrepresentation of His character and His Word. In honor of Jesus, we should develop habits that use God's Word to guide our behavior and conversations. As we lay down undesired habits and allow the Holy Spirit to develop the qualities of Christ within us, we will better represent Him to those around us.

First Peter 3:15 tells us, *But in your hearts set apart Christ as Lord. Always be prepared to give an answer to everyone who asks you to give the reason for the hope that you have. But do this with gentleness and respect.* As His followers, Christ asks us to be prepared to express the eternal hope we have in Him. There may be times when we receive direct questions about Jesus. For this reason, it's vitally important that each of us be capable of effectively sharing the gospel with anyone and at any time. (Training on this subject will be covered in the next chapter.)

In addition to direct questions, some questions could be considered as indirectly pertaining to Jesus. In this case, we should also be prepared to respond with comments that reflect our personal relationship with Him. For example, when others ask if you are having a good day, you could say, "Knowing Jesus makes every day worthwhile." Or, "The day has been challenging, but Jesus has been faithful to see me through." In another example, perhaps someone asks you about the weather. A possible Christ-centered response would be, "Isn't it amazing that the weather may catch us by surprise, but it never surprises God." Or, "It's wonderful to watch God meet our needs through both the sunshine and the rain."

Of course you will want to use words that are natural to your conversational style, but don't miss this point. Unless we are first prepared to direct people to Jesus, we may miss opportunities to do so. Begin listening to the questions others ask you. Then, ask God to provide you with answers that reflect His nature and His Word. Ask the Lord to use these conversations to cause people to continuously think about Him.

As we strive to point others to the person of Jesus Christ, we should also be sensitive to those who initiate conversations with us. For example, let's assume that as you wait for a doctor's appointment, the person next to you initiates a conversation. After sharing their grave medical condition, your response has potential to direct them to Jesus: "I'm glad you shared with me today. I want you to know that I will be praying for you." Or, "I realize these situations can be overwhelming. I will be praying for you because there is great power in prayer." Then, faithfully ask God to work mightily in the person's life. Also, communicating to the person how you'll be specifically praying for their needs may prompt them to think of Jesus as they experience answers to those prayers.

Listen Well

In addition to speaking effectively, another key element of relating well to others is being a good listener. James 1:19 instructs us to be quick to listen, slow to speak, and slow to become angry. In the same way we're to be careful to listen fully to what God and His Word have to say to us before responding, we should also choose to listen to others rather than responding too quickly.

Proverbs 18:13 teaches, *He who answers before listening—that is his folly and his shame.* Speaking before someone has completed their thought is impolite or even offensive. This is a poor habit for one of two reasons: either the person listening is presuming they know what the other person is thinking, or they believe their response is more important. This practice can also leave you misinformed, leading to an incorrect response. Instead, practice being a conscientious listener.

Think about it: How can we accurately implement biblical truth in a person's life without first understanding their point of reference? Luke 6:45 tells us that a person's mouth speaks from an overflow of their heart. This means that a person will most often speak what is actually in their heart. As we listen to what others are saying, particularly in response to Christ-centered questions, their heart attitude will be revealed.

This practice is enormously valuable in discipleship. It provides you with better comprehension of a person's spiritual condition. It also allows you to use the person's own words to help them consider any of their own thoughts that oppose truth. In addition, it gives you insight into the next steps necessary for them to walk in truth and reveals ways to pray for them. To best serve the needs of each individual, carefully listen to them while being sensitive to the Holy Spirit's discernment and flexible in allowing Him to guide your dialogue.

Also, be cautious about filling silent moments in conversation with speech. Instead, recognize these as occasions when the other person might be absorbing and contemplating the truth being presented. Be patient. These moments may be purposeful in prompting additional questions or thoughts. In order to be spiritually effective in the lives of others, our responses must reflect Christ's best. Therefore, ask the Holy Spirit to enable you to become a good listener and a patient responder, having His insight and timing.

Being a trustworthy listener will aid in building relationships and respect, resulting in others becoming more comfortable in communicating openly and honestly with you. Because we should be proven trustworthy, it's imperative that confidentiality is maintained in our relationships. However, there may be times when you're unable to keep information to yourself due to its content. For instance, a person may be in an abusive situation, has plans to harm themselves or someone else, or is involved in illegal activity. These circumstances need to be handled by professionals. For this reason, don't allow yourself to be caught off guard by someone asking you to keep a secret. Be prepared to explain your responsibility in the area of confidentiality.

For example, if a person asks to share something with you in confidence, kindly explain to them that you cannot agree to keep information a secret unless it is in their best interest. Help them understand that even though you would not share personal information with just anyone or without prayerful consideration, it may be necessary for them to have additional counsel or assistance.

Also be mindful that even though you are striving to be a good listener, you should not believe everything you hear. Therefore, choose to consistently test what you hear for truth by asking additional and more specific questions. This practice will be beneficial in gaining an accurate picture of a person's situation, which may be necessary in determining the best way to meet their needs.

As we become intentionally relational, as modeled for us through the life of Jesus, we'll become effective in representing Christ and His Word. Establishing and developing purposeful relationships will not always be easy. Yet, these lifestyle habits are necessary in furthering Christ's kingdom. Remember, Jesus promised to be with us always (Mathew 28:20). Therefore, as you practice being relational with the purpose of sharing truth, acknowledge His presence by relying on Him to meet your every need.

CHAPTER EIGHT

Sharing the Gospel

Before we can help others learn to walk in obedience to God's instructions, they must first hear and receive the gospel. For this reason, as we engage relationally with the purpose of sharing God's truth, we are to be mindful that the most important truth to convey is the gospel of His grace. In Acts 20:24 Paul stated, *"I consider my life worth nothing to me, if only I may finish the race and complete the task the Lord Jesus has given me—the task of testifying to the gospel of God's grace."* Is your life goal to consistently testify to the gospel of God's grace?

Some people dismiss opportunities to share the gospel because they aren't prepared to do so, are fearful of what others may think, or are uncertain if it will be received. Yet this fact still remains: Jesus has given us the responsibility of sharing the gospel (2 Corinthians 5:18). Are you embracing this personal responsibility? Rather than becoming deterred by the weight of following His request, rely on the Lord to teach you to become prepared and willing to testify to the gospel of His grace.

So, what is the gospel of God's grace? The word gospel refers to the good news or message of Jesus, and the good news of Jesus is found in God's grace. God's grace is His unearned, undeserved, unmerited favor; and the benefits of His grace are supernaturally powerful. Ephesians 2:8–9 says, *For it is by grace you have been saved, through faith—and this not from yourselves, it is the gift of God—not by works, so that no one can boast.* God's grace is His gift to those who believe in Him. If we could purchase or work to earn grace, we, rather than God, would receive the glory.

Grace is supernatural and supplies us with God's supernatural qualities, including His power (2 Thessalonians 1:11–12). God makes His grace available to us initially at salvation. He then continues to provide His grace, enabling us in every way to be triumphant over temptation and sin—transforming our lives into reflections of Jesus (Titus 2:11–14). When a person walks in the power of Christ, their life testifies to the gospel of God's grace!

Although God's grace is limitless and empowering in all ways (2 Corinthians 9:8), we must yield to its authority in order for it to be effective in our lives. When we desire to have our own way or assert our own will, we fail to acknowledge Christ's authority. In essence, we're saying, "No, thank you," to His equipping grace. As you continue to walk in the provision of God's grace by relying on its power, you will become increasingly effective in relating the gospel from a personal perspective.

The Goal of the Gospel

As you share the gospel, there may be times when you realize that the person you're talking with is unfamiliar with it. Perhaps their beliefs about the gospel may fail to fully align with Scripture. It is in these moments that recognizing any possible misunderstanding and pointing them to biblical truth becomes paramount. For example, some church leaders teach that the goal of the gospel is to "lead people to a point of salvation," often referred to as evangelism. Although the gospel is a powerful tool for evangelism, we should be careful that it doesn't become the end goal. If the end goal of the gospel becomes evangelism, discipleship can become secondary or, sadly, be overlooked all together.

Don't misunderstand: The Bible teaches that God specifically calls some of His followers to be evangelists, pastors, and teachers (Ephesians 4:11–13). But the distinction is in the unique roles designed for the body of Christ, not in the message. While a pastor's primary role is to use the gospel to shepherd a specific group of believers, an evangelist's primary duty is to spread the gospel to a wider audience. Isn't it exciting to know that God entrusts each of us with a specific role in building up one another in the faith? In pursuing this goal, we can each use the gospel to encourage others to develop from infants in Christ to maturity and fullness in Him (Ephesians 4:14–16).

The power of God's gospel enables people to be saved from sin and to walk in Christ's righteousness. This means that the gospel is to be shared with nonbelievers to encourage a relationship with Jesus and with Christ-followers to develop spiritual maturity. In Romans 1:16–17 Paul wrote, *I am not ashamed of the gospel, because it is the power of God for the salvation of everyone who believes: first for the Jew, then for the Gentile. For in the gospel a righteousness from God is revealed, a righteousness that is by faith from first to last, just as it is written: "The righteous will live by faith."*

As you can see, receiving the gospel is the starting point of salvation and discipleship, not the end goal. Otherwise, people may merely view Jesus as Savior, without acknowledging Him as Lord. Consider Romans 10:9–10: *If you confess with your mouth, "Jesus is Lord," and believe in your heart that God raised him from the dead, you will be saved. For it is with your heart that you believe and are justified, and it is with your mouth that you confess and are saved.* As ruler of all, Jesus requires His followers to believe in Him as Lord by continually relinquishing the control and authority of their lives to Him.

If receiving salvation were God's only goal, there would be no need for lordship. Philippians 2:12–13 tells us, *Continue to work out your salvation with fear and trembling, for it is God who works in you to will and to act according to his good purpose.* At the moment of salvation, God provides His indwelling Holy Spirit to each believer to work in and through them to accomplish His will. God's grace is worked out in a believer as they consistently relinquish personal control to the Holy Spirit, allowing Christ's power to have authority in their heart and life.

Our commission to make disciples also confirms this point: *"Go and make disciples of all nations, baptizing them in the name of the Father and of the Son and of the Holy Spirit, and teaching them to obey everything I have commanded you."* (Matthew 28:19–20). At the initial acceptance of God's grace, a person is made a disciple of Jesus. This is the starting point of a lifetime of discipleship. The next step of obedience is to be baptized in water, followed by continuing in the process of learning to obey everything God commands.

While some people have been led to believe that the end goal of the gospel is salvation, others have come to understand that it is merely a means of securing eternity with Jesus in Heaven. These people often reference John 3:16: *"For God so loved the world that he gave his one and only Son, that whosoever believes in him shall not perish but have eternal life."* Spending eternity in Heaven with Jesus will be wonderful. But, is this all the Bible is referring to when it uses the term "eternal life"?

In John 17:3 Jesus said, *"Now this is eternal life: that they may know you, the only true God, and Jesus Christ, whom you have sent."* Eternal life doesn't begin after we die. Eternal life is experiencing the benefits of God's grace now, through an abiding relationship with Jesus.

First Timothy 6:12 tells us, *Take hold of the eternal life to which you were called when you made your good confession in the presence of many witnesses.* When we accepted God's grace, we entered into a saving relationship with Jesus. We are then to continue to take hold of the benefits of eternal life afforded to us by developing an intimate relationship with Him. As you can see, when making disciples, it's of vital importance that we accurately understand and communicate the gospel of God's grace. The question then often becomes: What approach should be used when sharing the gospel with someone who is not a Christ-follower?

Great question! We know that genuine discipleship is based on the truth of God's Word and reliance on His Spirit rather than on a program. The aspect of communicating the gospel with the goal of initially making a disciple should be no different. As with any aspect of discipleship, the most effective approach is to be fully prepared to share the good news of God's grace and operate under the leading and authority of the Holy Spirit to do so. Then, leave the results to Him.

The Whole Gospel

As you anticipate sharing the gospel, you should also expect its message to make the lost world uncomfortable. After all, the good news of Jesus opposes the world's norms. Hearing the truth of God's grace often challenges people to reconsider their personal belief system. As a result, some people may become uncomfortable or even offended. Knowing this should motivate us to speak in love, while avoiding any temptation to soften or omit parts of the gospel message to make it more palatable.

When some people share the gospel, they focus on the blessings that result from following Jesus while overlooking the cost involved. Yet, this approach fails to fully represent the gospel. Consider this: When taking a test in school, students are taught that if any part of a true/false statement is false, the correct answer is false. Therefore, if a person claims an answer to be true that is partially false, they are deceived and have invested in faulty information. In the same way, a person basing their decision to receive Jesus on partial or faulty information may experience a false rather than a true conversion.

Let's look at this point further. Suppose there is an undetermined gas leak in an apartment building threatening the lives of its tenants. In order to save the residents from impending danger they must be warned. One rescue worker takes the approach of gently knocking on an apartment door. When the person comes to the door, he asks the resident to join him outside. He then explains the possible benefits of doing so: the tenant could take advantage of the beautiful sunshine, relax by taking a stroll, or perhaps even stop for ice cream along the way. The rescue worker then repeats this approach with other residents.

Based on this information, several of the residents choose to stay in their apartments. Others leave to enjoy the pleasures the rescuer had mentioned. But, when the sun gets too hot, the stroll is over, or the ice cream is eaten, they each return to their apartment still unaware of the impending danger. These people made their decisions based on potential personal pleasure rather than on the danger from which they needed to be saved.

At the same time, another rescue worker goes from apartment to apartment proclaiming to the residents that their lives are in danger. He tells them that, in order to be saved, they will need to flee from their current situation. Don't miss this point. Those who left the building based on this information realized it would cost them something: potential material loss, discomfort, or inconvenience. They chose to walk away from their current way of living for their greater well-being. In much the same way, we are like the rescue workers in this story. We hold the truth of God's grace that can save lives from eternal destruction. Rather than trying to persuade people with partial or incomplete truth, we should know the gospel message as it is presented in Scripture and fully share it.

Before going further, consider that becoming prepared to disciple is like filling your toolbox with many different tools. You do so because you can't be certain which ones you'll need for a particular job. Similarly, individuals may be in various places in their spiritual understanding. Since you may not know beforehand whom you'll encounter, it is important for you to become equipped to communicate every aspect of salvation.

Rather than become overwhelmed by this task, learn one biblical truth at a time. With this in mind, you may find it most beneficial to read through the remainder of this chapter, then go back and choose a particular subject matter to study until it becomes familiar to you. Commit your efforts to the Lord and rely on Him to enable you in every way to become a messenger of the gospel.

Unconditional Love: God's Motive

In explaining salvation, it's key for people to grasp the love of God and His redemptive plan for mankind. Unlike conditional love the world offers, God's love is not dependent on our actions or our love for Him. God loved each of us before we had knowledge of Him, despite our sinful state and failure to deserve such love (1 John 4:9–10).

God sent the perfect example of unconditional love to us through His Son, Jesus. Instead of the condemnation we deserve, Jesus accepted the penalty for our sin and, in return, made available to everyone His righteousness through grace. John 3:17 tells us, *"For God did not send his Son into the world to condemn the world, but to save the world through him."*

Be particularly sensitive to those who have experienced condemnation concerning their past choices or lifestyle. Perhaps they fail to see any hope of redemption. (Praise God for your testimony of God's grace and forgiveness, which resulted in your own salvation!) We can each assist others in recognizing Christ's redemptive love by conveying His truth in love, free of condemnation.

Love and Justice

In contrast to those who believe their deeds warrant no hope of salvation, there are others who believe that, since God is love, He won't condemn anyone to an eternal life in hell. However, John 3:16–18 shows that God's character includes both love and justice. Consider this: a man steals from numerous homes. He is eventually arrested and taken to a courtroom to appear before a judge. Because the man's actions prove that he is in violation of the law, the judge renders a guilty verdict. If the judge did not pass sentence or prescribe a penalty for the man's wrongdoing, we would view the judge as unjust. In the same way, we should not view God as unjust, but as just, when He requires obedience.

It's important to help others understand that God put His law in place, knowing that apart from Him we cannot keep it. Since He is just, God set the penalty for breaking the law as spiritual death or separation from Him. But, as a result of His great love for us, He also provided a way to avoid this penalty—our acceptance of Jesus' gift of grace.

A Free Gift

In sharing the gospel with the lost, it's important to explain that God's grace is undeserved and cannot be earned or purchased (Ephesians 2:8–9). This means that there is no available way to pay such a penalty; no amount of work or volunteer hours would merit atonement for one's sin. Because our culture is very achievement and task oriented, this truth is difficult for some people to grasp. Even so, a humble acceptance of this fact is fundamental to salvation.

Faith

We've learned that we are saved by grace through faith. Faith is defined in Hebrews 11:1: *Now faith is being sure of what we hope for and certain of what we do not see.* Faith is being certain or confident in the things of God regardless of whether they are visible. It then makes sense that if God asks us to believe only in those things we personally witness, our belief would not require faith.

Faith in Jesus is demonstrated in action, through trust and obedience to Him (Romans 1:17). This means that faith is active at the point of salvation and will be consistently prevalent in the life of a believer. For this reason, we should be prepared to help people realize that salvation comes through active faith in God, rather than through merely attending church, walking down an aisle, or repeating a prayer.

You may also find it beneficial to study Romans 3:21–26. In addition to providing a good summation of salvation, these verses also include subjects such as the Law, justification, and redemption which may also need to be addressed. We'll look at the meaning and significance of these words, as well as a few others, as we continue studying the process of salvation.

Repentance, Justification, Redemption

Salvation cannot occur without genuine repentance (2 Corinthians 7:10). Repentance results from sorrow over wrongdoing that leads to change in thought patterns and behavior. In order for us to be repentant of sin, we must first become aware of it in our lives. So, how do we recognize sin?

Consider this: Have you ever driven down a road without being aware of the speed limit? Once you see a speed limit sign, you realize it would be unlawful to travel over that particular limit. It isn't a feeling or an assumption, but the law that makes us aware of wrongdoing. In the same way, it's God's Law that makes us conscious of sin (Romans 3:20). Paul said that he would not have known what sin was except through the Law (Romans 7:7). Since people's ideas of right and wrong vary, it's only through looking at God's perfect Law that we learn of our imperfection due to sin.

Sin is what separates us from the righteousness of Holy God. No human can be declared righteous by fully observing the Law because we're incapable of doing so. Therefore, in order to be declared righteous and be restored to full fellowship with God, we must be justified. Justification is the word used to express our restored relationship with God and our rescue from sin and guilt.

Redemption is the means by which we're justified. Jesus' payment for our penalty of sin redeemed us from eternal sin and death. Our debt of sin wasn't cancelled, but paid in full through Jesus' death on the cross. Colossians 1:21–22 says, *Once you were alienated from God and were enemies in your minds because of your evil behavior. But now he has reconciled you by Christ's physical body through death to present you holy in his sight, without blemish and free from accusation.* Where sin made us enemies of God, acceptance of His grace pardons us from sin and allows us to be reconciled to Him.

Conversational Transitions

In preparing to share the gospel, equip yourself with ways to transition conversations from what is merely relational to focusing on God's grace. Asking Christ-centered questions can be instrumental in directing a conversation toward the gospel. For example, "What do you think about the subject of faith?" "Are you familiar with Jesus?" Or, "Have you ever thought about eternity?" As you anticipate opportunities to share your faith, pray for God to draw the hearts of the lost to Himself and enable you to share truth as He desires.

There may be occasions when God directs you to invite someone to accept His grace. In this case, ask God to open the person's heart to receive truth and to provide the courage and uninterrupted time to speak with them. The following sentences may be helpful in leading into a dialogue about salvation: "I hope you realize how much I care about you. I've been praying for you, and I'm concerned about where you might spend eternity. Can I talk with you about that?" Or, "I know you're very busy. But of all the things you have on your agenda that are pressing, the most significant thing on your list today should be to settle once and for all the subject of Jesus. May I help you do that?"

Responding to Positive Responders

Since people respond in diverse ways to the message of Jesus, it will also be beneficial to consider possible replies to various responses. For instance, after hearing the gospel, a person may tell you they want to accept Jesus into their life. Although this news can be exciting to hear, we should be careful never to assume a person's level of understanding.

In determining an individual's comprehension of the gospel, it's beneficial to ask open-ended questions rather than provide them with statements. For instance, "Accepting Jesus is the most important decision a person will ever make. What does that decision mean to you?" Or, "What difference do you think accepting Jesus will make in your life?" Listen carefully to their answers. Then, confirm clear comprehension of truth and clarify any misunderstandings by kindly pointing them to Scripture.

Delayed Receivers

After hearing the gospel, the person may respond by demonstrating clear understanding of that truth, yet choose to delay placing their faith in Jesus at that time. If God leads you to address their response, lovingly point them to the truth found in 2 Corinthians 6:2: *"In the time of my favor I heard you, and in the day of salvation I helped you." I tell you, now is the time of God's favor, now is the day of salvation.* God is gracious and wants everyone to be saved (1 Timothy 2:4). But a person can never know how many opportunities they may have to receive God's gift of grace. In a situation such as this, continue to ask the Lord to draw the person to Himself.

Rejecters of Truth

If a person refuses to place their faith in Jesus due to rejection of that truth, it may be helpful to share Hebrews 10:26–27. Kindly explain that, since there is only one sacrifice for sins, the alternative for not believing in Jesus is eternal separation from God. Then, pray that the Lord will reveal truth to this person's heart and mind. Although it will be worthwhile to equip yourself with these additional truths, remember to only share as God allows and leads.

Evangelistic Follow-Up

God may also direct you to participate in evangelistic endeavors in which an invitation is given for people to discuss questions they have or decisions made in response to hearing the gospel. Because this role could have enormous spiritual significance, ways to effectively relate to those who respond to the gospel, through evangelism, are covered in the appendix of this book.

Regardless of when the Lord provides opportunities to communicate the gospel, obedience is reflected in how well we're prepared to share and our willingness to do so. If you're not already sharing the gospel with others, take time to practice doing so. You may want to prepare an outline of verses to have on hand, or mark specific verses in your Bible for quick reference. (A simple outline of Bible verses to use in presenting the gospel is provided in the appendix of this book.) Ask the Holy Spirit to enable you to memorize the most significant verses concerning salvation. Then, ask a family member or friend to allow you to practice communicating the message of God's grace.

Rather than instruct His disciples to invite lost people to hear Paul or someone else preach the gospel, Jesus commissioned each disciple, as He does today, to share the gospel message—it is our privilege and highest purpose.

CHAPTER NINE

Results of Salvation

As we live each day in anticipation of sharing the gospel, we should also anticipate some people accepting God's gift of grace in our presence. If you're with someone when they accept Jesus, they may not feel any different. So it's worthwhile for them to understand some of the changes that have already taken place. For example, it's an amazing truth that upon acceptance of Jesus, as Savior and Lord, the Holy Spirit takes up residence within the individual's body. First Corinthians 6:19–20 says, *Do you not know that your body is a temple of the Holy Spirit, who is in you, whom you have received from God? You are not your own; you were bought at a price. Therefore honor God with your body.*

In the Old Testament prior to Jesus' life, death, and resurrection, King Solomon built a temple for God. Upon completion, God's presence filled the temple. In the New Testament, after Jesus' return to heaven, God provided every believer with the indwelling presence of the Holy Spirit. This is why a believer's body is referred to as a "temple of the Holy Spirit." A believer acknowledges their body as God's temple by honoring Him in what they say and do. These verses also remind us that, in order for sin to be forgiven, a great price had to be paid. Convey to new believers that each of our lives is of great worth to God, evidenced by the price Jesus paid to redeem us.

Second Corinthians 5:17 explains, *Therefore, if anyone is in Christ, he is a new creation; the old has gone, the new has come!* It's important to communicate that God's plan of salvation provides us with a new nature, enabling us to conform to His image through the powerful work of the Holy Spirit. Although a new believer must learn and grow in this new nature, the desire to do so will be evidence of genuine salvation (1 John 2:3–6). Also, it's important to point new believers to Scripture that explains the assurance and confidence that is theirs through the indwelling Holy Spirit (Ephesians 1:13–14; 1 John 5:13).

Even though one who has experienced salvation is a changed person, they may not sense or recognize an immediate difference in their life. Assure new believers that God calls us to walk by faith rather than by feelings or intuition. While God has created change within the believer's heart, He also wants to create change in their life by conforming them to His will. This transformation is a process and doesn't occur overnight.

Paul provided encouragement for us in Philippians 2:12–13: *Continue to work out your salvation with fear and trembling, for it is God who works in you to will and to act according to his good purpose.* Out of reverence for Christ, Paul urged fellow believers to continue to respond in obedience by choosing to grow in their relationship with the Lord. He then reminded them that such work is achieved only through the enabling of the Holy Spirit. We, like Paul, can encourage new believers to rely on the Holy Spirit to develop obedience in their lives.

NOTE: The Bible teaches that one of the first steps of obedience for a new believer is to be baptized in water. God also instructs His disciples to participate in the ordinance of Communion. Since you may have the privilege of discipling new Christ-followers, it will be beneficial for you to be prepared to communicate the significance of both water baptism and Communion. These subjects are included in the appendix of this book.

In making disciples, we should be prepared to communicate the difference between those actions God deems necessary for salvation and those that are essential for us to continue in obedience. Because Scripture teaches that salvation precedes water baptism and Communion, consistently communicate that these ordinances are to be followed in obedience to Jesus' instructions and are not contributors to salvation. Through participation in both water baptism and Communion, a believer thankfully acknowledges Jesus' death and celebrates their new life in Christ.

CHAPTERS 10 THROUGH 14

THE PROCESS OF A GROWING DISCIPLE

CHAPTER TEN

Promoting Spiritual Growth

A thorough life-transforming work begins when a person receives Jesus' gift of grace. It's important, at this point, to distinguish those works that are complete in Christ Jesus at the moment of salvation, from those that will require our continual involvement or response in the transformation process. For example, Hebrews 7:27 tells us that Jesus made one sacrifice of Himself on the cross, for all. His payment for each of our sins, past, present, and future is a completed and finished work. Second Corinthians 5:21 says, *God made him who had no sin to be sin for us, so that in him we might become the righteousness of God.* It is through the gift of salvation that we receive God's grace and are forever reconciled to Him. At the point of salvation, each believer is also sealed with the Holy Spirit, guaranteeing their inheritance (Ephesians 1:13– 14). This means that our salvation is eternally secure.

Yet, the Bible also teaches that we are to work out our salvation

(Philippians 2:12). In other words, our participation will be necessary in further experiencing the grace of God. This doesn't mean, however, that the work will be ours. Rather, we will need to continue to respond, through surrender, to God's amazing, transforming work.

God's Spirit resides within each believer because genuine transformation occurs from the inside out. Attempting to develop change through any other means is merely an effort to modify behavior. Think about it. At salvation, God provides us with His Spirit which is an immediate and complete work. But He doesn't give us new bodies, minds, or emotions. These elements that, in the past, governed our old way of life will be transformed to reflect Jesus as we continually yield to God's will. As this transformation process takes hold in every area of our life, God receives the glory for the work His Spirit is achieving. If we fail to allow the Lord to perform His transforming work, we will continue to operate in our old self instead of in our new nature.

So, how do we make certain we are faithfully allowing the thorough work God desires to achieve in our lives? We do this by learning to consistently respond in obedience to the teaching of God's Word and His Spirit's training. Only then can we assist others in developing the same transforming spiritual disciplines in their lives.

As you continue to study this book, pay attention to the significance of the foundational order and detail in God's instructions. Also significant is His design for your participation in the transformation process, through the practical application of each principle. As you study each biblical truth, pause to consider whether or not it is consistently being practiced in your daily life. If the principle is not practiced, ask God to show you why not and to teach you how to begin implementing it in practical ways. Then, rely on His Spirit to enable you to follow through.

As we grow in our own spiritual development, we are also to be encouraging the spiritual maturity of others. For this reason, the following chapters also provide practical assistance in encouraging others to faithfully follow Jesus. As you prepare to train others in discipleship, it's valuable to realize that the choice to grow spiritually is both individual and personal. This means that our responsibility lies in promoting spiritual growth while leaving the results to God. It's very freeing to know that God requires that we each be accountable for our own obedience, not the obedience of others.

The following chapters also contain the words *mentoring*, and *disicpling* when referring to *making disciples of Jesus*. Although the word *mentor* or the phrase *one who disciples* are not used in Scripture, examples of this type of relationship are found throughout the Bible (Moses and Joshua, Naomi and Ruth, Elizabeth and Mary, Jesus and His disciples, Paul and Timothy, etc.) Today, some believers avoid forming mentoring or discipling relationships because they are uncertain of what they should look like, while others develop programs to group people together without a clear spiritual objective or training. As defined by examples in Scripture, these relationships were intentional and purposeful in teaching, guiding, and training others to walk daily by faith in the truth of our Lord Jesus Christ. Today, we, too, can intentionally and effectively invest in the lives of others to promote spiritual maturity.

CHAPTER ELEVEN

Teachability

In the United States and other parts of the world, knowledge of Scripture is consistently available through the Bible, credible Christian books, television programming, and technology. But, how do we convert knowledge of Scripture to understanding of truth that leads to personal application? In order to receive understanding of truth with the intent of applying it, we must become teachable. God's Word then presents us with a choice of whether or not to obey Him by implementing truth in our daily lives.

Psalm 119:33–34 says, *Teach me, O LORD, to follow your decrees; then I will keep them to the end. Give me understanding, and I will keep your law and obey it with all my heart.* Do you recognize the Psalmist's desire to be teachable, and his purpose to gain understanding and obey truth?

Consider this: Is there a difference between a person being approachable and a person being teachable? A person who is approachable may be friendly and even engaging in conversation.

However, those qualities don't necessarily make them teachable. Someone who is teachable is willing and open to learn. In other words, a person becomes spiritually teachable when they desire to receive and apply truth. If we're not careful, we can allow ourselves to be approachable without ever becoming teachable.

What does being teachable have to do with spiritual growth? Since we can't obey what we don't understand and can't gain understanding without first being teachable, becoming teachable is essential to spiritual growth. Sadly, a person who is consistently approachable without ever becoming teachable may fail to thrive spiritually. Would others consider you to be teachable, desirous of learning all God has to teach you with the intent of obeying?

Available Knowledge

↓

Choice to Be Teachable

↓

Choice to Receive Understanding

↓

Choice to Obey by Applying Truth

↓

Resulting in Life Transformation

In order to continually experience spiritual growth in our lives, we must become teachable and remain so. James 1:22 tells us, *Do not merely listen to the word, and so deceive yourselves. Do what it says.* God's desire is that each time we're presented with the truth of His Word (whether through reading on our own, a group Bible study, individual discipleship training, hearing a pastor's sermon, etc.), we would receive what is said in our head and apply what is said with our heart. Because the heart is where genuine change occurs, apart from heart application there will be no change.

Since God wants us to consistently develop spiritual maturity, consider the following practical steps to aid you in becoming teachable.

- Ask God to give you a heart that is teachable, willing to learn spiritual truths, and desirous of pleasing Him.
- Before reading the Bible, ask the Holy Spirit to enable you to gain personal understanding.
- Prior to arriving at church or Bible study, ask the Lord to prepare your mind to focus on truth and make your heart ready to receive it.
- Ask Him to provide you with examples for personal application and the strength to live them out.

By inviting God to be an active part of our spiritual growth, we're preparing our hearts and minds to be focused on truth and open to receive what He has for us. Unless we prepare to receive the things of Christ, we can easily become distracted by the busyness or hurry of the day, the difficulties of life, and the people around us. As a result, the opportunity to hear, receive, and apply truth can easily be lost. Plan to become teachable in the days ahead by practicing the principles we've looked at.

In discipling others, ask them to consider whether someone else can make them teachable, and then discuss each person's personal responsibility for gaining knowledge and understanding. It may be beneficial to explore reasons people aren't teachable. For example, a person may say he doesn't enjoy reading, or considers himself to be too old to learn new things. John 5:17 tells us, *Jesus said to them, "My Father is always at His work to this very day, and I, too, am working."* Show the person you're mentoring that, because God is continually at work around us, He has something to teach us about Himself throughout each day.

Then, discuss avenues through which they can learn from Him: God's Word, His creation, and personal experiences. Remind them that God may have something new to teach them through familiar things like Bible stories heard during childhood, or favorite hymns and praise songs. Since Scripture conveys the importance of being teachable (Psalm 51:6; Proverbs 3:13–14), encourage those you mentor to become teachable, and pray that God will enable them to do so.

CHAPTER TWELVE

A Call to Surrender

As you become increasingly aware of the importance of being teachable, it will also become evident that teachability is a fundamental aspect of surrendering one's life to Christ. In addition, surrendering one's life to the Lord is fundamental to personal discipleship. Let's consider the significance in linking these two elements together: Teachability is a position of openness to learning and accepting God's will, with the intent of following it. Being teachable is inviting the Lord to reveal His truth to the deepest parts of our lives, with the aim of being transformed into His image. When a person chooses to surrender their life to Jesus, they move from merely being teachable to actually yielding their life in obedience to the transformation process.

Jesus is the perfect example for us of a fully surrendered life. In John 12:23–25, Jesus is speaking of His personal surrender to the will of God the Father through His upcoming death on the cross: "*The hour has come for the Son of Man to be glorified. I tell you the truth, unless a kernel of wheat falls to the ground and dies, it remains only a single seed. But if it dies, it produces many seeds. The man who loves his life will lose it, while the man who hates his life in this world will keep it for eternal life."*

Jesus is reminding His disciples that unless a kernel of grain dies, it fails to fulfill its intended purpose to produce fruit; it merely remains an individual seed that eventually decays. The Lord's willingness to surrender His life through death on the cross produced eternal life for those who would believe in Him. When we die to self through wholehearted surrender by following and serving Jesus, He generates new life in us.

We learned, through our study of the gospel, that Jesus Christ is both Savior and Lord (Romans 10:9). When a person recognizes that Jesus died for their sins, acknowledges that they are a sinner in need of repentance, and asks Jesus to forgive them of sin—they are, according to Scripture, saved. At this point Jesus becomes their Savior, redeeming them from the eternal penalty of sin and death. Yet Scripture also teaches that salvation requires confession and personal recognition that Jesus is Lord. This means that a person acknowledges and accepts Jesus' authority by allowing Christ to rule in their heart and life. Therefore, laying down one's life through surrender, or dying to self, is evidence of genuine regeneration.

As you can see, acknowledging Jesus as Savior without personal surrender to His Lordship creates conflict because, according to the Bible, a person can't live for both Christ and self. Romans 8:5–8 tells us, *Those who live according to the sinful nature have their minds set on what that nature desires; but those who live in accordance with the Spirit have their minds set on what the Spirit desires. The mind of sinful man is death, but the mind controlled by the Spirit is life and peace; the sinful mind is hostile to God. It does not submit to God's law, nor can it do so. Those controlled by the sinful nature cannot please God.*

Notice that there are only two options: choose to live according to the sinful or worldly nature, or choose to yield to the control of God's Spirit. The Spirit's desires have nothing in common with the desires of the world. Therefore, if we choose to live apart from God and according to our sinful nature, we're choosing to block the Holy Spirit from controlling selfish desires. It's really that simple.

So, what does a life completely surrendered to Christ look like? Second Corinthians 5:15 says, *And he died for all, that those who live should no longer live for themselves but for him who died for them and was raised again.* To fully surrender to Christ is to voluntarily relinquish any right to self-will in order to follow God's will.

Surrender is not a one-time event but a moment by moment intentional choice. As we increasingly lay down personal plans and agendas to follow God's will, His presence and power are revealed in our lives. On the other hand, if we fail to surrender to Christ's will, we will continually struggle in disobedience, confusion, and doubt. Is there any area of your life that you're striving to control rather than yielding it to Jesus? Is there anything keeping you from fully surrendering to Him? If so, choose to lay it down in obedience to the Lordship of Christ.

In Galatians 2:20, Paul gave us a wonderful word picture of a life fully surrendered to Christ Jesus: *"I have been crucified with Christ and I no longer live, but Christ lives in me. The life I live in the body, I live by faith in the Son of God, who loved me and gave himself for me."* Paul made a conscious choice to give up his own pursuits for the sake of Christ by no longer recognizing his life as his own. This means that even though he continued to dwell in his physical body, Paul no longer allowed his flesh, or sinful nature, to have control.

Christ asks the same of His followers today. For example, rather than asserting our right to make decisions independently, we are to surrender to God's will by inquiring of Him and following His lead. Instead of holding on to anger that has the potential to result in resentment and bitterness, we are to surrender the personal hurt to God's control, asking Him to enable us to forgive and restore. It is through the daily practice of surrendering one's life that Christ's nature is revealed and God is honored.

Before further exploring the subject of surrender, let's pause to consider what the drawbacks would be to giving God control of our lives. In relinquishing authority to Christ, we choose to cease entertaining self-centered thoughts or pursuing selfish desires. Rather than assert a human prerogative to have our own way, each surrendered life will consistently seek God's will and obey Him. A life surrendered to the Lord Jesus will not resemble the world or easily fit in with those who pursue a worldly standard.

Now let's think about the potential benefits of allowing God complete control and authority over our lives. As we walk in accordance with the Spirit, rather than in the flesh, we will develop a lifestyle that is pleasing to God. Likewise, we will gain victory over temptation and sin while avoiding unnecessary guilt and regret. Through yielding to God's will instead of to selfish desires, we will bring honor to Jesus and point others to Him. A life fully surrendered to Christ experiences peace, freedom, and contentment rather than internal confusion and conflict.

Some people like having a sense of control in their lives. However, in reality, only Almighty God is in charge of all things. Therefore, we shouldn't become swayed by life situations appearing to be in our control, nor be overwhelmed by those outside of it. Each time we choose to surrender our lives to God's authority we acknowledge that He is in charge. If it is not already your practice, begin today relinquishing full control to the Lord; trusting His way is best.

Then, be encouraged by the promises found in Jeremiah 17:7–8: *"Blessed is the man who trusts in the LORD, whose confidence is in him. He will be like a tree planted by the water that sends out its roots by the stream. It does not fear when heat comes; its leaves are always green. It has no worries in a year of drought and never fails to bear fruit."* Although the word *blessed* appears early in this passage, the blessing received from the Lord comes after a person's act of trust. Surrendering your life to Christ is a daily act of trust. As we grow in reliance on the Lord, our lives bear fruit by bringing honor and glory to the name of Jesus.

The following exercise may assist you in better recognizing and embracing personal surrender to the Lordship of Jesus. Begin by thinking of words that you would use to categorize various aspects of your life such as *family, job, church, friends, school, commitments,* and *activities.* Next, write these words on a piece of paper in the order in which you would prioritize them. You may choose to prioritize these items however you like (in the order of importance, their required time commitment, etc.).

As you examine the prioritized list, consider how subtle the world's way of thinking can be. For instance, the world would tell us that in order to maintain happiness in our lives we need to keep our priorities in order. Using this theory, if our job has a higher priority than our families and we're unsatisfied, moving our families into a position of higher priority would make them and us happier. But that isn't necessarily true, especially for the long term. Some people find that their priorities shift based on such things as work and family commitments, or friends' momentary needs. This makes an objective evaluation of priorities difficult because they're in constant flux.

In order to view our priorities objectively, we're going to need to consider our lives from God's perspective. God desires to have authority over every aspect of our life and honoring Him as our number one goal in everything we do (Matthew 22:37). In order for God to have authority, we must be personally surrendered to Him. Consistently yielding to the Lord enables us to become more aware of His presence and prevents us from excluding Him from portions of our day. This means that, rather than striving to maintain a particular order of the various aspects of our lives, we will surrender to God's authority in each area.

GOD	GOD	GOD	GOD	GOD	GOD
Family	Job	Church	Friends	School	Commitments

Now, stop to reconsider the various aspects of your life by listing the details that are associated with each of them. Include the Lord in this process by asking Him to reveal to you those specific people and activities He wants included in each list. For instance, while prayerfully considering the makeup of your family, the Lord may lead you to write down each of the names of your family members. Under the subject of "job," He may prompt you to note the names of your boss, co-workers, and particular duties required of you. Repeat this process until each list is complete.

When you have finished the lists, ask yourself the following questions for each entry: Does Christ have first place in this part of my life? Have I given God full authority and control over this area of my life? How is this relationship or activity honoring to Him? Most importantly, am I willing to surrender completely to God's authority, allowing Him to teach me and change anything about my life He deems necessary? Because our loving God wants to do a thorough work in our lives, choose to be sensitive to the prompting of His Spirit and allow the necessary time needed to complete this exercise. Ask the Lord to reveal His will concerning each specific area and obediently make any changes God shows you to make.

Keeping in mind that God's desire is for each of our relationships and activities to be under His authority and centered in His will, a portion of this exercise might look like the following:

Let's presume that some co-workers found out that you enjoy softball and invited you to join their team. Because you desire to be a witness to them, you accept their invitation. Initially, the team plays one night a week. Then they begin playing two nights a week and out-of-town weekend tournaments, taking you away from valuable time with family and the fellowship of the church.

You would begin by writing "softball" and the list of individuals on the team. Then, ask God to show you His will concerning this activity and the people involved using Christ-centered questions: "Did I ask God to reveal His will to me prior to my participation with this team?" "Is my placement on this team pleasing to the Lord?" "Is God in control of this area of my life or is the activity taking control?" (Be aware that even though it may be your heart's desire to witness to your co-workers, this may or may not be the Lord's avenue in which to do so.)

Next, ask the Holy Spirit to reveal any changes that need to take place concerning the specifics of this activity and the people involved. Then, follow through with the instruction He gives you. Because God wants to achieve a thorough work in our lives, take the time to inquire of Him concerning each activity and person on your list.

This exercise can be beneficial as a tool for periodic self-evaluation. In the process of self-evaluation, those areas of our lives that are pleasing to God will result in peace. On the other hand, those areas that aren't in line with God's will may result in conviction that prompts us to initiate a change in behavior or direction. A consistent willingness to embrace God's desired life changes is an indication of a surrendered life.

In discipling others, it's important to demonstrate a life that is surrendered to the Lord Jesus. Remember, those areas of your life that you fail to yield to Jesus reflect an unsurrendered life. Those unsurrendered areas will not only stunt personal growth, but can also risk causing others to stumble who may be following your example.

Teach those you mentor that authentic discipleship requires sincere surrender. Ask them to consider the appropriate personal response to Jesus' amazing gift of mercy displayed in the forgiveness of their sins. Then, read Romans 12:1: *Therefore, I urge you, brothers, in view of God's mercy, to offer your bodies as living sacrifices, holy and pleasing to God—this is your spiritual act of worship.* Help them see that a "living sacrifice" is one who, although physically alive, has put an end to selfish desires. The sacrificing, or putting to death, of our sinful nature is increasingly achieved as we consistently relinquish control to the Holy Spirit.

Then, if they haven't already done so, encourage each person you disciple to surrender control to the Lord, giving God full authority to reign freely in their heart and life. Further explain that, regardless of the biblical truth being taught, obedience always involves surrender to the Lordship of Christ. Just as Jesus' life was fully surrendered to God the Father for His glory, we, too, should be fully surrendered to Jesus in honor of Him.

CHAPTER THIRTEEN

Sanctification

In order for believers in Jesus to follow His will, they must first recognize it. In 1 Thessalonians 4:3, we learn that it is clearly God's will that we be sanctified, consecrated to His higher purpose. A simple definition of the word sanctify is "to be set apart to God."

Romans 6:6-7 tells us, *For we know that our old self was crucified with him so that the body of sin might be done away with, that we should no longer be slaves to sin—because anyone who has died has been freed from sin.* At the point of salvation, Jesus forgives our old way of life and provides us with everything necessary to live a new life in Him. We're then freed from sin in order to pursue righteousness.

As we pursue righteousness, we continue to lay down old selfish habits and sinful behaviors, exchanging them for new ones that reflect God's holiness. This is often referred to as the process of sanctification. Even though we're freed from sin, we need to learn to walk in that freedom. In other words, this new way of living doesn't automatically establish itself; it must be learned.

Are you recognizing a significant link between personal surrender to Christ's Lordship and sanctification? Look at Romans 6:9–13: *For we know that since Christ was raised from the dead, he cannot die again; death no longer has mastery over him. The death he died, he died to sin once for all; but the life he lives, he lives to God.*

In the same way, count yourselves dead to sin but alive to God in Christ Jesus [surrendered to the Lordship of Christ]. *Therefore do not let sin reign in your mortal body so that you obey its evil desires. Do not offer the parts of your body to sin, as instruments of wickedness, but rather offer yourselves to God, as those who have been brought from death to life; and offer the parts of your body to him as instruments of righteousness* [separated from sin, set apart to God]. As we become increasingly surrendered to God's will, we're being sanctified unto Him. Is it your heart's desire to be set apart to God as an instrument of righteousness?

In John 17:15–17, Jesus was speaking to God the Father concerning the way His disciples would be sanctified. He said, *"My prayer is not that you take them out of the world but that you protect them from the evil one. They are not of this world, even as I am not of it. Sanctify them by the truth; your word is truth."*

Since Jesus wants us to impact this lost and dying world for His kingdom, He doesn't want us to be isolated from it. For this reason, we must be able to affect the world without being affected by its evil. Let's think about it. If we isolate ourselves from people who live in opposition to Christ, how can we expect to influence them for Jesus? On the other hand, if we allow ourselves to fit into this world, our deeds will look just like those of every other person.

Unless a line is drawn in our lives that sets us apart for righteousness, others will not question our deeds, nor recognize them as being of

God. In what ways are you guarding against the temptation to remove or isolate yourself from the world rather than becoming sanctified while living in it? When you recognize the temptation to fit in by mirroring the world's way of thinking, speaking, and behaving, how do you respond?

God asks us to be set apart for His will because it represents His best for us. This means that God doesn't want us to merely settle for the good in life, but He desires us to pursue godliness. The world has led us to believe that some things appearing to be good can also be considered godly. This is why Jesus tells us to use biblical truth as the standard in determining those activities and behaviors that are godly as well as those that are not.

Ephesians 4:22–24 says, *You were taught, with regard to your former way of life, to put off your old self, which is being corrupted by its deceitful desires; to be made new in the attitude of your minds; and to put on the new self; created to be like God in true righteousness and holiness.* Sanctification begins with a mindset that desires to intentionally follow truth. We progress in the process of sanctification as we learn to distinguish the lies presented by the world from the truth of God's Word. Then we walk in truth as it applies to each aspect of our life. In doing so, we lay down old selfish desires and sinful habits and replace them with new ones that reflect God's nature.

Since biblical truth is the absolute standard for godly living, conforming to any other standard will fail to produce righteousness. To put it simply, the only way we can be truly set apart to God is through personal application of His Word. Consequently, we are to use truth as the dividing line between good and godly behavior.

The following illustration depicts good versus godly behavior.

Remember, being sanctified is not only separating ourselves from sin (as noted by the line on the left below), but it is also setting ourselves apart to God for His purposes (indicated by the line on the right). Choosing to draw lines in our lives to separate those things that reflect biblical truth from those things that do not will be instrumental in our pursuit of righteousness.

It's not enough to merely live near sin while striving to avoid it or abstain from it. To set ourselves apart to Christ is to intentionally forsake sin, in order to pursue righteousness by consistently implementing godly behaviors. Be mindful that setting yourself apart from sin may be good, but setting yourself apart to Christ is a godly pursuit! (The arrow, in the diagram above, signifies lives committed to the process of sanctification by consistently moving in the direction of Christlikeness.)

Rather than settling for what could be considered "good," we are to acknowledge God's best by pursuing godliness. For example, let's presume that God has convicted you of spending too much time on the computer or watching T.V. Merely spending less time involved in this activity wouldn't be enough to achieve sanctification. You would also need to examine how God would want you to spend that time, and then fill the time accordingly. In another example, let's say that you're with a group of friends who are gossiping about another person. Rather than merely abstaining from the slanderous conversation by not joining in, you can pursue sanctification by asking them to stop gossiping or by choosing to walk away.

Sanctification is an ongoing work by the power of the Holy Spirit and involves every aspect of our lives. Although pursuing personal righteousness is a process, those who are following Christ will experience progress in the process. In 1 Thessalonians 5:23–24 Paul is encouraging fellow believers: *May God himself, the God of peace, sanctify you through and through. May your whole spirit, soul and body be kept blameless at the coming of our Lord Jesus Christ. The one who calls you is faithful and he will do it.* It's wonderful to know that, although sanctification requires participation on our part, the actual work is God's. Just as Almighty God is the means by which we're saved, He is also the means by which we're sanctified.

In discipling others, questions concerning specific choices and behaviors pertaining to sanctification will most likely be asked. Rather than just considering the answers to the questions being asked, train others to ask the right questions. For example, sometimes a person will want to know how far they can move or act in a particular direction without it being considered sin. However, for one who desires to be sanctified, this line of thinking is incorrect. When thinking correctly, a person would ask, "How can I move closer to Christ?" By asking questions from a godly, rather than a worldly, perspective a person can be encouraged to make choices that reflect a life that is sanctified.

In another example, a believer asks for assistance in determining whether a particular action would be acceptable. Remember, an action that may appear good may not be godly. In this case, teach the person that Christ-followers should choose God's absolute best for their lives instead of those things that are merely acceptable or satisfactory. Training others to use truth in making choices will aid in helping them to set themselves apart to God.

Even so, there are things that the Bible doesn't specifically prohibit. Therefore, we are to personally search the deep truths of Scripture and rely on the discernment of the Holy Spirit to determine the Lord's will in specific areas of behavior. Isaiah 48:17 tells us, *This is what the LORD says—your Redeemer, the Holy One of Israel: "I am the LORD your God, who teaches you what is best for you, who directs you in the way you should go."* Encourage those you disciple that, as they walk ever closer with the Lord, He will reveal His best path for their lives, one step at a time.

In addition, followers of Jesus are to take into consideration the effect their personal choices may have on the lives of others. First Corinthians 10:23–24 says, *"Everything is permissible"—but not everything is beneficial. "Everything is permissible"—but not everything is constructive. Nobody should seek his own good, but the good of others.* Show others that some life issues aren't a matter of whether or not they can or have the right to participate, but whether or not they should participate, based on the spiritual well-being of themselves and others.

Remind each person you disciple that the Holy Spirit is always available and willing to work to conform us to God's image. However, since the Spirit will never force change, we must be taught to willingly allow Him to do so. This is achieved by choosing to activate our faith.

CHAPTER FOURTEEN

The Significance of Faith

God's Word tells us that those who pursue righteousness will live by faith (Romans 1:17), and that without faith it's impossible to please God (Hebrews 11:6). Sometimes people refer to themselves as persons of faith, but what does being a person of faith or a person who is faithful look like according to Scripture?

To answer this question, let's remind ourselves of the meaning of faith. Faith is having confidence in and certainty of the eternal things of God regardless of physical proof (Hebrews 11:1). In other words, faith is the settled surety that God is who He says He is and will do what He says He will do. People sometimes indicate that they're walking by faith when taking some sort of blind leap. However, biblical faith isn't blind. On the contrary, a person who walks by faith in God is consistently focused on His character and promises regardless of whether they're visible.

Can you imagine how different life would be if God continually provided us with physical proof to reassure us of His truth? Following

Him wouldn't require faith and would result in a lack of personal reliance on Him. Taking into consideration the definition of faith, would you say it's your habit to trust in Christ by faith or invest in the appearance of circumstances?

One of the keys to continually walking by faith is having an understanding of how it's established and developed. The Bible teaches that Jesus is the author and perfecter of our faith (Hebrews 12:2). This means that faith has its origin in Jesus and is further developed, or perfected, as we grow in our relationship with Him. Living by faith is a lifelong endeavor for those pursuing righteousness.

Since applying principles of faith can be enormously life-changing, let's walk through them slowly.

Grace: God's Gift and Provision

We know that Jesus paid the full penalty for all past, present, and future sin, making His death on the cross a complete and finished work (1 Peter 3:18). This means that everything Jesus needed to do to provide us with daily victory over circumstances, temptation, and sin has been accomplished! As a result of this work, those who believe in Jesus receive God's gift of righteousness and provision of grace (Romans 5:17). Don't miss this: It is by grace that we're saved and it's by grace that we continue to receive victory over circumstances, temptation, and sin.

Colossians 2:9-10 says, *For in Christ all the fullness of the Deity lives in bodily form, and you have been given fullness in Christ.* To put it simply: everything needed to achieve victory is found in Christ Jesus, and those who believe in Him have been given the fullness of Christ. It's as if God's eternal, limitless grace has been deposited to each and every believer and is just waiting to be withdrawn (2 Corinthians 9:8). All we need to do is learn to tap into it.

Grace: Accessed through Faith

So, how do we access this amazing gift of grace? This is where faith comes in. We know that when we initially received Christ's gift of salvation it was by grace, through faith (Ephesians 2:8–9). In the same way, through faith we continue to access God's grace.

In 2 Thessalonians 1:11–12, Paul wrote to Christ-followers: *We constantly pray for you, that our God may count you worthy of his calling, and that by his power he may fulfill every good purpose of yours and every act prompted by your faith. We pray this so that the name of our Lord Jesus may be glorified in you, and you in him, according to the grace of our God and the Lord Jesus Christ.* Notice the significant order in these verses: Access to God's enabling power is prompted by our faith. As we rely on God's power through faith, our lives are transformed and His glory is revealed. (If we continue to strive to live in our own strength, the best we can do is modify behavior.) Is it your desire to continually access God's enabling grace?

Paul was familiar with God's grace at work in his life, especially in the midst of suffering. In 2 Corinthians, chapter 12, we learn that he pleaded with the Lord to remove the source of his suffering. In verse 9 Paul wrote, *But he [Jesus] said to me, "My grace is sufficient for you, for my power is made perfect in weakness." Therefore I will boast all the more gladly about my weaknesses, so that Christ's power may rest on me.*

Paul, like us at times, pleaded with the Lord for his situation to change so that he might experience victory. But instead, Jesus provided Paul with His grace, knowing it was more than sufficient. Rather than embrace defeat, Paul was able to find joy in his shortcomings, persecutions, and adversity because they provided opportunities for God's power to be revealed in him.

A Life of Active Faith

Now that we've settled the issue that grace is accessed by faith, how do we consistently nurture and activate our faith? Scripture teaches that faith comes from hearing the message of truth concerning Jesus (Romans 10:17). Jesus' message, including His thoughts, promises, and instructions, is revealed in the Bible (John 1:1–2). As we read, meditate on, and study God's Word, we're spending time with Jesus, thereby nurturing our faith. Be aware, however, that there is a distinction between nurturing our faith and activating it.

In 1 Thessalonians 2:13, Paul provides a wonderful word picture of a life of active faith: *And we also thank God continually because, when you received the word of God, which you heard from us, you accepted it not as the word of men, but as it actually is, the word of God, which is at work in you who believe.* (Emphasis added.) God produces faith in us as we hear the Word of God, accept it as absolute truth, and choose to believe what it says. We then activate our faith by walking moment by moment, trusting in God's truth that enables each of us to supernaturally experience victory.

Let's look at these principles further from a practical perspective. God's Word is continually available to us. As we place ourselves in a teachable position, God will give us understanding of what application of His Word would look like in our daily lives. But up to this point, we've not yet put God's Word into practice. This means that even though we may have been nurturing our faith, it is not yet activated. In other words, we can have biblical knowledge and understanding while lacking personal application. While in this state, God's grace waits to be accessed.

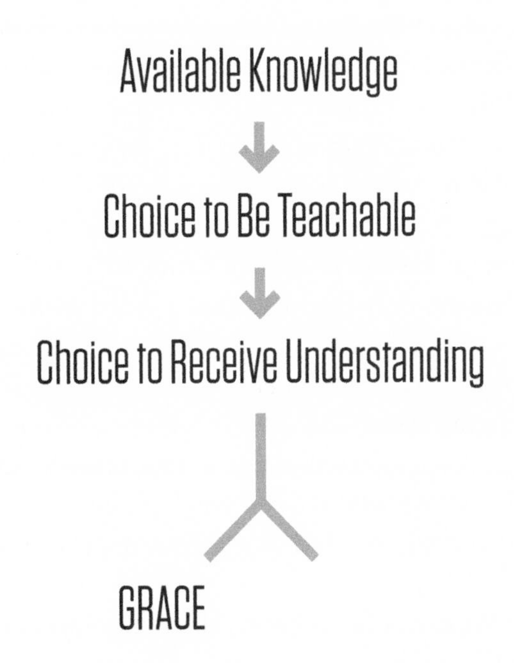

Faith: A Trust Issue

Then circumstances and the numerous variables associated with life enter into the picture. Each one presents us with a fork in the road—a moment of decision; and life is full of them. Don't miss this point: How we view life situations will determine whether or not we walk by faith. We will either focus on the circumstance and base our decisions on what we see, hear, and feel, or we will walk by faith through reliance on God's truth. The significant difference lies in merely listening to God's Word without also trusting in it: hearing, but failing to put it into practice.

Look, once again, at James 1:22–25: *Do not merely listen to the word, and so deceive yourselves. Do what it says. Anyone who listens to the word but does not do what it says is like a man who looks at his face in a mirror and, after looking at himself, goes away and immediately forgets what he looks like. But, the man who looks intently into the perfect law that gives freedom, and continues to do this, not forgetting what he has heard, but doing it—he will be blessed in what he does.*

This is a significant passage to use in learning to walk by faith. Notice that the person who only listens to God's Word without practicing what it says is self-deceived. How can this be? Although a person may have a sense of accomplishment from reading, meditating on, or talking and singing about God's Word, without personal application no genuine transformation will result. On the other hand, James 1:25 tells us that the person who is intentional in looking at God's Word and puts it into practice will be blessed. How does this happen?

Consider this: We can either presume about our physical appearance or look into a mirror, knowing that it will reveal our true reflection, including personal imperfections. Then the decision is ours whether or not to change our physical appearance. (Note, the mirror only reveals the needed change. It doesn't make the change for you.) In a much similar way, God uses His Word to reveal our true heart condition. We can either presume about our spiritual well-being or we can intentionally look into God's Word, allowing it to reflect our spiritual condition. Then the choice is ours whether or not to apply revealed truth in our lives (by faith, through the power of God's Spirit) or determine our own direction (by sight, through investing in human thoughts and desires).

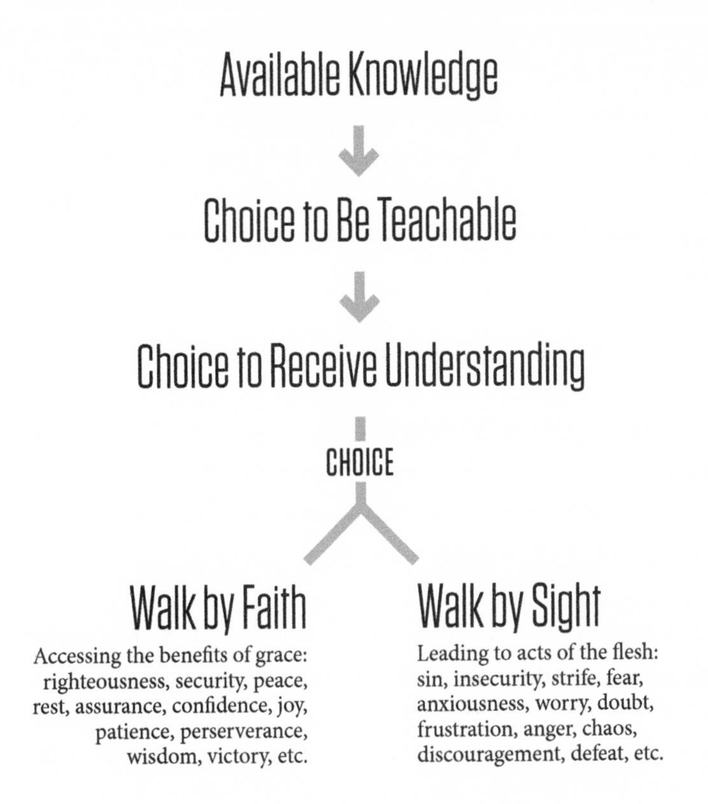

Living by faith is choosing to continually put to death the things of the flesh in exchange for trust in God's truth and the benefits of His grace. A life of faith, through reliance on Jesus, enables us to experience security rather than insecurity, peace instead of turmoil, confidence instead of doubt, victory rather than defeat. If we settle for the things of the flesh, we experience consequences that fail to reflect God's grace and create separation between ourselves and the things of God.

Since living by faith is much different from depending on personal knowledge, perceptions, or emotions, it must be learned and requires a lifestyle change. For example, it may be that God shows you that it's necessary to change the way you think in order to align your thoughts and actions with His truth. At times, He may prompt you to change the way you feel about a situation in order to consider His perfect perspective. Because we can never stay where we are while simultaneously moving in the direction Jesus is leading us, a life of faith will require personal change.

Even though people may desire to experience the benefits of a transformed life in Christ, they may also be reluctant to embrace the transformation process and the changes required to achieve spiritual victory. In other words, they want the results without committing to the process. Is it your habit to readily embrace the changes necessary to produce a lifestyle of righteousness in you?

In order to embrace change, it is valuable to first recognize specific inclinations that lead to the avoidance of change. By defining these, you can better identify moments of temptation. Then, in each moment, victory can be achieved by placing your faith in Jesus rather than giving into the inclination to follow the flesh or defaulting to old behavioral patterns.

In the remainder of this chapter, we will examine reasons for reluctance in implementing spiritual change in our lives. Invite the Lord to reveal to you any predispositions that cause you to avoid personal change. Consider the possible effects these have on your way of thinking and behaving. Then, ask the Holy Spirit to enable you to take the necessary steps to gain victory in your pursuit of righteousness.

Change Can Be Overwhelming

Sometimes the mere thought of change can be overwhelming,

especially if our minds are focused on creating the change in our own strength. Instead of becoming overwhelmed, we should activate our faith by depending on the power of the Holy Spirit to do the work in us (Philippians 2:12–13).

The original disciples recognized their inability to achieve the high standard of righteousness God set for them. Rather than becoming overwhelmed, they asked Jesus to increase their faith (Luke 17:5). Jesus taught them that the faith He provides is more than adequate to accomplish what God asks of each of His followers; we need only to exercise it. When tempted to invest in thoughts and feelings that could overwhelm us, we should rely on Christ's faith to work in us. Because faith only comes from Jesus, He in turn receives glory for the transforming work.

Change Can Be Difficult

We may view a change in lifestyle as difficult, especially if we've developed set behavior patterns over an extended period of time. Thinking that change is too hard may cause us to be reluctant to adjust our lives as God desires. Although it's true that change can be challenging, nothing is too difficult with God.

Hebrews 13:20-21 says, *May the God of peace, who through the blood of the eternal covenant brought back from the dead our Lord Jesus, that great Shepherd of the sheep, equip you with everything good for doing his will, and may he work in us what is pleasing to him, through Jesus Christ, to whom be glory for ever and ever. Amen.* Rather than concede to a challenge, we can live by faith, trusting Almighty God to do the work in and through us. In doing so, we become victorious!

First John 5:3-5 tells us, *This is love for God: to obey his commands.*

And his commands are not burdensome, for everyone born of God overcomes the world. This is the victory that has overcome the world, even our faith. Who is it that overcomes the world? Only he who believes that Jesus is the Son of God. What an amazing promise: Victory in Jesus is not just available, but is fully obtainable through faith in Him! By allowing God to enable you to embrace change, rather than avoid it, His will is accomplished in your life and He receives the glory.

Change Can Be Uncomfortable

As we pursue righteousness, we will continually be presented with a choice. Regardless of the situation, that choice is always the same—whether or not to obey the Lord. If you're not already walking according to truth in a particular area of living, the choice to obey God will require change. Repentance, which leads to obedience, is God's word for change. The Holy Spirit consistently convicts our hearts of wrongdoing in order to produce repentance. However, conviction can make us uncomfortable and at times can even be painful. Why is that so often true?

Our human nature wants control. Submitting to God's authority by allowing Him control can make us uncomfortable or ill at ease. A desire for control reflects the flesh, whereas a desire to surrender to Jesus reflects faith. Ask God to enable you to recognize those occasions that tempt you to take matters into your own hands and to change you by giving you the desire and strength to surrender to His will.

The other reason that conviction can make us uncomfortable is due to pride. Our human nature can be prideful by wanting to be right or by being unwilling to admit to wrongdoing. Laying down our desire to be right, in order to become righteous, goes against our human will, creating discomfort. Sometimes when we experience discomfort through conviction, we'll attempt to excuse or justify an action or behavior.

However, in order to maintain a right relationship with Jesus, we must be consistent in forsaking sin rather than excusing it.

Be careful. In trying to justify disobedience, we can deceive ourselves about our truly sinful condition (1 John 1:8). Because God's Word and His character are perfect, we must conform to His definition of righteousness rather than to our own. Develop the habit of asking God to show you when you make excuses for sin and for His help in making the necessary changes in your behavior.

In addition, learn to appreciate conviction—yes, genuinely appreciate it. Read Hebrews 12:10–11: *Our fathers disciplined us for a little while as they thought best; but God disciplines us for our good, that we may share in his holiness. No discipline seems pleasant at the time, but painful. Later on, however, it produces a harvest of righteousness and peace for those who have been trained by it.* Even though God uses conviction to make us uncomfortable by prompting us to change, repentance restores our relationship with Him. Therefore, rather than avoiding the discomfort of conviction, embrace it by immediately following the Holy Spirit's lead, and then rejoice in the peace obedience provides.

Change in Uncertain Times

Lacking direction for the future can also cause us to feel uncertain and reluctant to implement change. Since life is filled with uncertainties, we should follow God's directives to activate our faith as prescribed in Proverbs 3:5–6: *Trust in the LORD with all your heart and lean not on your own understanding; in all your ways acknowledge him, and he will make your paths straight.* These verses hold powerful instruction: If you want God to guide your life, you will need to trust fully in Him. This means that you'll continually pursue His will rather than invest in your own limited understanding.

God tells us to live by faith, rather than by sight, because faith reflects His perspective; whereas sight is merely human perspective (2 Corinthians 5:7). To put it simply, faith equals God's perspective; sight equals man's perspective. Our human nature can cause us to make choices based on the appearance of circumstances or on available information. But, in doing so, we can easily lose sight of God's best path for us.

Psalm 32:8 says, *I will instruct you and teach you in the way you should go; I will counsel you and watch over you.* God will never ask us to walk this journey of faith alone, but will be with us each step of the way. We learn to walk in step with God as we practice following His counsel. Since we can't always see physical evidence of the work Christ is achieving, obediently following His direction will only occur through faith. Acting on anything else would be faulty and uncertain.

God will consistently allow unknowns in our lives to give us opportunity to exercise our faith. In each case, we are to practice placing each speculative thought and concern at the feet of Jesus. We choose to actively wait on the Lord by asking Him to reveal His perfect wisdom and discernment regarding everything committed to Him. Then, we are to move in the direction God is leading, trusting that He knows best.

Change Can Be Costly

Implementing God's desired change in our lives could require any number of things: time, effort, money, etc. When considering potential changes necessary for walking in obedience to Jesus, it can be tempting to think only of the requirements without considering all the possible benefits. Doing this may cause us to focus on the cost of obedience rather than on its many blessings, resulting in a hesitation to embrace change.

Read through Psalm 19:7–11 and identify the words that describe the benefits of God's instructions. *The law of the LORD is perfect, reviving the soul. The statutes of the LORD are trustworthy, making wise the simple. The precepts of the LORD are right, giving joy to the heart. The commands of the LORD are radiant, giving light to the eyes. The fear of the LORD is pure, enduring forever. The ordinances of the LORD are sure and altogether righteous. They are more precious than gold, than much pure gold; they are sweeter than honey, than honey from the comb. By them is your servant warned; in keeping them there is great reward.* Rather than focusing on the cost, ask God to enable you to have a mind set on the blessings of obedience.

Are you more clearly recognizing situations that tempt you to walk by sight rather than by faith? Because faith is essential in creating permanent change in our lives, we should value its importance and live by its principles. As you disciple others, be mindful that undesired habits and behaviors you are unwilling to change in your own life may validate undesired behavior in the lives of others. Therefore, ask the Lord to enable you to embrace change as you apply the principles of faith.

In discipling others, help them grasp the significant benefits of a life lived by faith. Be sensitive to responses that reflect the potential hesitancy of a person to change, and be prepared to respond with truth. For example, a person tells you that they are worried about a situation in their life. They then ask you to help them identify what God might want them to do. You listen carefully to their explanation of the situation and respond with pertinent Scripture. They then reply, "Oh, I just hope I can quit worrying." What does the person's response tell you?

Their words reveal they lack the intent necessary to receive or apply truth. So, what happened? The problem with scenarios such as these is this: the person sought godly counsel but failed to apply truth. Therefore, they will experience neither change nor victory. As a result, they will mistakenly think or feel like God's Word has disappointed them.

In order to experience consistent spiritual growth, a person must be continually willing to change. While making disciples, we should encourage each person to embrace the truth being presented. In the previous situation, the person's response suggests that the presented truth did not take immediate hold and, therefore, we can't be certain of its effectiveness.

When a person's response reveals a lack of application, prayerfully consider following up with a question or comment similar to one of the following: What do you think might prevent you from worrying? Do you think worrying is a choice? Please tell me what you plan on doing with the truth I shared with you. Because a person must first recognize a need to change before they alter their life, be patient in assisting others to see a need for change. Then, follow God's lead in encouraging them to implement changes necessary to achieve obedience. As a person experiences the blessings that follow obedience, they will become less hesitant to embrace change.

If you are mentoring a person who says they want to live by faith, yet is reluctant to implement changes that reflect a life of faith, it may be beneficial for you to suggest a personal study of Hebrews 11. In this chapter, God provides numerous examples of people who obediently followed Him regardless of personal cost. Encourage the person that following wherever God leads and permitting Him to implement His desired changes reflect the lifestyle of a genuine disciple.

Since nothing is impossible with Christ, we can each experience life with unlimited possibilities as we place our faith in Him. As we trust more fully in His promises and His nature, the Lord will prove to be faithful. As a result, we will experience an increase in personal faith.

CHAPTERS 15 THROUGH 24

THE PROCESS OF APPLYING TRUTH

CHAPTER FIFTEEN

The Significance of Applying Truth

Before continuing our journey, let's take a few minutes to review the stops we've made thus far and their significance. We've learned that at the moment of salvation a believer receives the fullness of Christ—everything necessary to produce godliness. A disciple then grows in their relationship with Jesus by consistently placing himself in a teachable position, willing to learn God's will. He then follows the Lord's will by continually surrendering personal desires to pursue God's directives. The Bible refers to this supernatural transformation process as sanctification. We become increasingly sanctified as we choose to live by faith in Jesus.

Because faith is nurtured and developed through the truth of Jesus, life application of His principles is of utmost value to the life of a disciple. In other words, life application results in transformation.

We know that absolute, infallible, eternal truth comes only from God (John 1:14). God reveals truth through His Word (John 17:17) and His character found in His Son, Jesus (John 1:17), and in discernment provided by His Spirit (John 14:16–17, 26). It can be helpful to simply remember it this way: Truth is revealed through God's Word, His nature, and His Spirit. Since God's truth is absolute, these three elements will never contradict each other. For example, if the thoughts you experience aren't in line with Scripture or the character of Jesus, you can be confident that these thoughts are not from the Holy Spirit (1 John 4:1).

Jesus graciously provides us with His perfect Word and the enabling of His indwelling Spirit so we can understand and obey it. This brings us to our next significant question: Is there a difference between studying the Bible and studying the Bible for personal application? (The answer is yes!)

Through study of the Bible we can gain knowledge. But when we choose to study the Bible with the purpose of applying it to our hearts and lives, we intend to actually use what we learn to allow the Holy Spirit to transform us. So, does this mean that there is a difference between receiving God's Word and receiving a word from God? (Again, the answer is yes.)

God's Word, the Bible, is applicable to all subject matter. Our practical God uses His Spirit to reveal to our hearts and minds ways to personally apply His Word in everyday living. For example, the Bible teaches us to love our neighbors. We receive this truth by agreeing to put it into practice by conveying love to our neighbors. But how do we show Christ's love to so many unique individuals? Only through the discernment of the Holy Spirit. It is God's Spirit that reveals to us specific ways to demonstrate love to each individual in a manner that will reflect Jesus and draw others to Him.

Since personal application of truth is vital to spiritual success, the next nine chapters will provide you with tools to accurately apply truth and practice godly principles. Consider for a moment how important it is to be aptly equipped with tools. For example, my husband is a carpenter. When we were first married, there would be occasions when he would ask me to retrieve a tool from his toolbox. I didn't always know the name of the tool, what the tool looked like, or what it was used for. But the important point was that I knew where to find it. As I became more familiar with my husband's tools, I could not only identify them by name and their purpose but also could use them effectively.

The same can be true for our spiritual lives. God alone holds every tool to equip us, in every way, to succeed in life. He wants us to use the tools He provides to apply, or put into practice, His truth. As you consistently practice biblical principles, they will become habits and eventually a lifestyle. God desires to continually teach us new things about Himself and His Word, thereby making application of truth a lifelong process.

The Necessity of Application

Remember, truth is revealed through God's Word, His nature, and His Spirit. To experience transformation, we must learn to take God's Word from the pages of Scripture and rely on His Spirit to apply it to our hearts and lives—converting godly principles into godly behavior. Therefore, as we study God's Word, it should ultimately be for the purpose of personal application.

Let's review together James 1:22–25: *Do not merely listen to the word, and so deceive yourselves. Do what it says. Anyone who listens to the word but does not do what it says is like a man who looks at his face in a mirror and, after looking at himself, goes away and immediately forgets what he looks like. But the man who looks intently into the perfect law that gives freedom, and continues to do this, not forgetting what he has heard, but doing it—he will be blessed in what he does.* Notice that the deception of the person who merely listens to the word of God is self-induced (vs. 22). In contrast, the person who chooses to be a doer, one who applies God's Word, looks at it with the intention of following it; resulting in blessing (vs. 25).

Exposure to God's Word powerfully provides us with an image of our true spiritual condition. If our intent to follow God's will is sincere, we'll receive His truth and rely on His strength to diligently implement it in our lives; producing change. As a result, God promises to bless our obedience. Sadly, if we only read or listen to God's Word and fail to understand and apply it, we become deceived.

The religious leaders in Jesus' day present an example of people who were deceived. They had firsthand knowledge of the Scriptures and had witnessed God's power in both the presence and miracles of Jesus. Yet, they failed to receive the truth of Jesus for themselves. They became deceived because they failed to trust in and rely on God's truth. Jesus rebuked them for their lack of applied truth in Matthew 22:29. Jesus replied, *"You are in error because you do not know the Scriptures or the power of God."* Jesus desires for each of His followers to live in victory rather than in error that leads to deception.

Be careful. Self-deception can occur more easily than you may think. For example, on occasion people quote a portion of Scripture from John 8:32: *The truth will set you free.* However, truth without application fails to produce transformation that results in freedom. To put it simply, just knowing the truth is not enough to set you free.

Let's reread the portion of Scripture in its greater context. John 8:31–32 says, *To the Jews who had believed him, Jesus said, "If you hold to my teaching, you are really my disciples. Then you will know the truth, and the truth will set you free."* Belief in Jesus is the first step to discipleship. Those who "hold" to His teaching, by continually following Jesus' instructions and trusting in His promises, experience His transforming work in their lives. This consistent practice of personal obedience and perseverance in Christ results in true freedom from the Law, temptation, and sin.

It's essential that we not only be diligent in applying truth in our lives, but we must also be applying it correctly. Consider for a moment some of the basic properties of math—the properties of addition. Based on appearance, these properties are merely sentences. Yet, when applied to an equation, these properties help us quickly arrive at the correct answer. For example, the Commutative Property of Addition explains that when two numbers are added, the sum is the same regardless of the order of the addends. The property can be practically applied like this: $6 + 2 = 2 + 6$. Consequently, we can confidently expect that when we add two of the same sets of numbers together, regardless of the order, the sums are equal. However, if we were to apply the same property when adding two unlike sets of numbers, we could be in error ($6 + 2 \neq 3 + 4$). (Error results when we attempt to apply a specific property incorrectly or fail to apply it at all.)

In a similar way, Scripture verses are trustworthy sentences. When they're applied accurately to situations and circumstances, they enable us to come to correct answers or conclusions for godly living. On the other hand, if God's principles are misapplied, partially applied, or not applied at all, the result is spiritual inaccuracy.

It's interesting to note that the principles of addition never fail, even though their use and application may differ according to each equation. The same is true for God's truth. It never fails (Psalm 119:160), although it's use and application may differ according to each situation.

In discipling others, please be mindful that genuine spiritual transformation, resulting in victory, is only experienced through personal application of God's Word and reliance on His power. Knowledge of this truth should motivate us to slow down and help others evaluate individual situations and potential wrong thinking in light of biblical truth, and guide them in practical ways of applying it. This means that, rather than merely providing encouraging words or quoting Scripture, we will show others what God's Word says, what it means, and how it can be applied to help them experience victory.

Be aware that some people who claim to be Christians will also contend that their Christianity doesn't always work for them. Because God's Word is infallible, these assertions are often the result of a personal lack of application or misapplication of truth. For this reason, it's extremely important that we are diligent in correctly understanding and applying biblical principles throughout our daily routines. As your personal application of Scripture becomes commonplace, others will learn to effectively apply truth through your example.

Facing Opposition

Because God's truth is in total opposition to the world, the Bible teaches us that those who walk according to truth will encounter spiritual warfare. Walking by faith in God's Word is instrumental in furthering Christ's kingdom and a definite threat to the enemy's goals. Our Mighty God encourages us to contend for our faith (1 Timothy 6:12) and will enable us to be victorious in each battle we face.

In 2 Corinthians chapter 10, Paul explained how each of us can consistently experience Christ's victory. He began in verse 3: *For though we live in the world, we do not wage war as the world does.* We each have a physical presence in this world. Yet, as believers, we're to recognize each battle as being spiritual. This means that we cannot successfully oppose the enemy by our own means and should, therefore, avoid engaging in spiritual warfare from a worldly perspective. In other words, rather than battling in the flesh using human means, we're instructed to use the power of God's truth to destroy that which opposes Christ.

Paul explained further in verses 4 and 5: *The weapons we fight with are not the weapons of the world. On the contrary, they have divine power to demolish strongholds. We demolish arguments and every pretension that sets itself up against the knowledge of God, and we take captive every thought to make it obedient to Christ.* Did you catch that? God's Word has divine power to completely demolish anything that comes against us!

Therefore, in order to be prepared for spiritual warfare, we must learn to practice abiding in truth. While God's grace makes victory available, application of truth makes victory obtainable!

Throughout each day, you encounter information in various forms such as media, entertainment, the Internet, conversations, and even personal thoughts. Not all information we encounter represents the truth of God's Word or His character. If we entertain thoughts that are contrary to truth, we risk weakening our strong defense against the enemy. For this reason, we should develop the habit of evaluating information in light of truth. If the information reflects God's truth, then we should choose to invest in it by living accordingly. If it fails to mirror truth, then we should refrain from embracing it.

Now, consider the information you receive from those closest to you. Although family members and friends may think they have our best interest at heart, unless their guidance lines up with biblical truth, it is merely opinion or theory and shouldn't be accepted as truth. In these cases, you can lovingly communicate to family and friends your desire to fully follow God's Word and rely on His power to accomplish His will.

This can also apply to the emotions we experience. Although our personal feelings may be very real, they don't always reflect truth. Therefore, it's necessary to take emotions captive that oppose God's Word, holding them powerless to have any effect on us. This takes practice. Begin today to develop a lifestyle of relying on God's power to take captive each thought and emotion that opposes Christ. Next, exchange them for truth and walk in obedience to Him.

In discipling others, teach them that the enemy will not be pleased with their commitment to live in complete reliance on God's Word and His power. Consequently, the enemy will do his best to distract them from being effective for Christ's kingdom. Help them to recognize that one way the enemy will try to distract them is by tempting them to invest in things that oppose God rather than walking in His truth.

Help those you disciple be aware of the reality of spiritual warfare and God's desire for us to be victorious in battle. Discuss the difference between encountering information and receiving it, and challenge them to be proactive by only embracing truth. Train them to be mindful that it's not enough just to be prepared to apply truth; they must actually be doing it moment by moment each day. It is in these moments that they will choose to stand on biblical principles or invest in speculative thought. They will either walk in truth or settle for the thoughts and feelings of the flesh.

CHAPTER SIXTEEN

The Power Source

God's power enables us in every way to accomplish His will. Consider these amazing truths: Through His power God spoke the world into existence, restores the dead to life, and calls things that are not as though they were (Romans 4:17). Absolutely nothing is impossible with God (Luke 1:37).

In Ephesians 3:16–19, Paul prayed that each believer may experience Christ's supernatural power. In verses 20–21 he said, *Now to him who is able to do immeasurably more than all we ask or imagine, according to his power that is at work within us, to him be glory in the church and in Christ Jesus throughout all generations, for ever and ever! Amen.*

Imagine for a moment what it would look like for you to consistently involve God's power in your daily life, experiencing what you once considered to be impossible. Imagine victory over temptation, sin, and circumstances, resulting in God's glory being revealed now and to the next generation. What would it take for you to move from imagining abundant life to actually experiencing it?

God promises that we can each experience victory in this life (1 John 5:3–5). However, there is a vast difference between victory that is available and victory that is obtained through Jesus Christ. Victory through the power of Jesus is continually available, but is only obtained and experienced as we choose to rely on Jesus' power through an abiding relationship with Him.

In the same way we learned to abide in Christ by evaluating our heart motives and by receiving His wisdom, discernment, and direction in chapter 5, we are to continue to abide in Jesus by operating in His strength. Reliance on God's power enables us to practically apply all His Spirit reveals to us as we remain connected to Him. We can think about it this way: We wouldn't merely plug an electronic device into an electrical outlet to have the appearance of being connected to the outlet. We would plug the device in with expectation that the power source we've connected to will enable the device to operate effectively for our benefit. Similarly, we are to live expecting that, as we plug into Christ's power, He will fulfill His promise to enable us to experience victory in all things.

We also apply God's power in our lives by relying on His authority over life's circumstances and His strength to secure victory. Because the victory will be achieved through Him, rather than through our own efforts, Christ will receive the glory, making us effective for His kingdom.

First Corinthians 4:20 tells us, *For the kingdom of God is not a matter of talk but of power.* We could speculate for hours about the expectations of a particular electronic device without ever experiencing its potential. We realize what it's actually capable of when it receives power. The same can be true for us spiritually. We can earnestly discuss the possible application of God's Word, yet fail to apply it through His strength. Even though we are fully equipped in every way to do

God's will, we must choose to stay connected to Christ Jesus, our power source, in order to operate at our full potential.

As we are trained to stay connected to the power of God's Word, His nature, and His Spirit, it is also significant to understand that these elements are very much entwined. For example, we've learned that, in order to walk in obedience to God, we must consistently read, understand, and apply Scripture. As we remain connected to or abide in Jesus, He empowers us—He gives us the desire to read His Word, the ability to comprehend it, a heart to receive it, understanding to apply it, and the strength to obey it—producing victory. That's powerful!

The Power of God's Word

In order for us to grow in our reliance on Scripture, it's valuable for us to grasp its trustworthiness. The Bible contains the very words of God. Second Peter 1:20–21 says, *Above all, you must understand that no prophecy of Scripture came about by the prophet's own interpretation. For prophecy never had its origin in the will of man, but men spoke from God as they were carried along by the Holy Spirit.* The Bible wasn't written as the result of any human effort and does not in any way represent human theories, opinions, or philosophies.

God's Word carries with it His power, and only God's power provides victory over sin and death (Romans 1:16). Consequently, it's of great significance that we learn to abide in Christ's Word, allowing it to dwell within us (Colossians 3:16). This means that we are to become so familiar with Scripture that truth is continually brought to our hearts and minds.

It only makes sense that the amount of power we apply, or make use of, will be dependent on the amount we've withdrawn from the power source. We know that God's Word is continually available to each of us and His truth applies and equips us for any situation (2 Timothy 3:16–17). However, if we have not equipped ourselves with the knowledge of God's Word prior to a circumstance, we have nothing to draw from or apply. Sadly, defeat rather than victory may result.

For example, as we make decisions throughout each day, we base our conclusions on what we know or on knowledge we acquire. Some decisions need to be made immediately without further investigation, so these decisions are made based on the current knowledge we have. In order to avoid the trappings of sin in these moments, we must be able to make choices and judgments based on personal knowledge of biblical truth.

Having God's Word merely available to us is similar to a person having a state-of-the-art kitchen appliance, equipped with every amenity imaginable. However, if they choose to ignore the instructions by failing to plug it into a power source, they can end up assuming that the appliance doesn't work, resulting in great disappointment. Similarly, we can be disappointed by assuming God isn't working in our lives when in actuality we haven't read His instructions and aren't "plugged in" to His power. As we learn to rely on the trustworthiness of Scripture, we will realize its power.

Psalm 119:97–99 says, *Oh, how I love your law! I meditate on it all day long. Your commands make me wiser than my enemies, for they are ever with me. I have more insight than all my teachers, for I meditate on your statutes.* Here, the Psalmist communicates the benefits of abiding in truth by meditating on Scripture throughout each day. In what ways are you daily meditating on God's W ord?

By consistently meditating on Scripture, you will be able to commit it to memory. Psalm 40:8 tells us, *"I desire to do your will, O my God;*

your law is within my heart." Psalm 119:11 says, *I have hidden your word in my heart that I might not sin against you.* These verses provide insight into the significant link between knowing God's Word and walking in God's power. Make no mistake. We'll never be able to overcome the world's temptations apart from the power of God in our lives. This is why the Psalmist chose to hide God's Word in his heart—so that he would recognize truth and then rely on God's power to overcome sin.

In discipling others, explain the significance of having an intimate, abiding relationship with the Lord and train them to develop a lifestyle that relies fully on Christ's power for all things. (Prior to doing so, it may be helpful to review chapter 5: The Significance of Abiding.) Then, encourage them to abide in God's Word.

Since biblical truth has nothing in common with the world's way of thinking, we can't be saturated by the world and recognize truth. Therefore, train others that before spiritual victory can be achieved, they must continually transform their way of thinking by renewing their minds with truth. Romans 12:2 says, *Do not conform any longer to the pattern of this world, but be transformed by the renewing of your mind. Then you will be able to test and approve what God's will is—his good, pleasing and perfect will.* As we abide in God's Word, our minds are transformed into thinking according to truth. By using biblical truth, we can test and approve God's will. These tools, when applied, transform a life from living according to the pattern of this world to a life controlled by the power of God's Spirit.

Encourage others to pray that God will reveal to them moments to spend in His Word, and challenge them to avoid filling these occasions with other activities. Also, ask them to consider some practical ways to consistently meditate on and memorize Scripture, and help them to formulate a plan for success in doing so. It can be beneficial, when learning to meditate on God's Word, to begin reading a single verse of Scripture each morning. Then, review that same verse throughout the day. It can also be valuable to select verses that apply specifically to a current circumstance or need in one's life, and then post them in obvious places.

Train others to memorize God's Word by repeatedly writing or typing a specific verse of Scripture. They may find it beneficial to review verses on their computer or cell phone for consistently meditating on or memorizing. As situations arise in their daily lives, they can draw from and apply God's powerful Word stored within them to achieve victory!

Even though memorization is naturally easier for some people than others, God will enable every believer to succeed in committing to memory His truth. For this reason, encourage those you mentor to ask God to help them in this endeavor. If the person desires accountability in this area, you may suggest a verse for them to memorize and provide them with an opportunity to repeat the verse to you. In addition, remind them to gain understanding of each verse or passage of Scripture being memorized, thereby facilitating correct application.

The Power of God's Nature

The Word of God is consistent with His character: absolute, eternal, flawless, and infallible. John 1:1–2 says, *In the beginning was the Word, and the Word was with God, and the Word was God. He was with God in the beginning.* Not only has God and His Word existed since time began as we know it, but they are also one and the same. When we spend time in God's Word, we're spending time with God. Learning the characteristics of God enables us to recognize His powerful qualities that are continually available to us. Even though as humans we may become weak and weary, God's renewing strength enables us to remain strong (Isaiah 40:29–31). Is it your habit to rely first on the Lord's strength rather than your own or that of others?

Although we may fail in our own strength, God's strength never fails; it is only through His powerful work within us that God's will is fully accomplished. When a person rejects the use of God's power, the Lord may allow him to carry out his actions to some form of completion. However, those actions will have no eternal value, nor will they be under the guidance and protection of Christ (John 15:5). Sadly, those who choose to walk in their own strength, rather than remaining in Jesus, set themselves up to experience eventual defeat and miss victory. Again we can see that we must be a willing participant by choosing to plug into God's supernatural power in order to achieve His will.

In discipling others, it can be valuable to engage them in dialogue to consider the following questions: Are you aware of the Spirit's presence and available power through the moments of your day? Are you consistently tapping into God's power through an abiding relationship with Him? Then, encourage each person to ask the Lord to make them aware of His constant presence and their need for Christ's power.

To further promote an abiding relationship with Jesus, it may be beneficial to have the person consider their daily routine of personal tasks and appointments. For instance, they might leave home to go to work, stop working to have lunch, leave work to pick up their children, etc. Then explain that just as they find each day comprised of their involvement in a series of tasks, they should live each day abiding in Christ as a continuation in His presence, all the while bringing to mind His powerful attributes and His desire to be involved in each aspect of their day.

It is a great privilege that, regardless of where we are or what we may be doing, we can continually dwell in the presence of the living God. As a result of our great need for the Lord's power every moment of every day, our response should be to avail ourselves of Him. This will take practice. For this reason, encourage those you disciple to focus on the benefits of abiding in Jesus. As they experience the benefits of God's power for themselves, they will desire to grow ever closer to Him.

The Power of Prayer

We gain respect, trust, and dependence on the Holy Spirit's power through consistent communication with Him. In Ephesians 6:18, Paul tells us to pray in the Spirit on all occasions with all kinds of prayers and requests. To "pray in the Spirit" is to acknowledge, through communication, God's authority by submitting to His will (Galatians 5:25). Praying in accordance to the will of the Spirit allows God to be the predominant authority in our lives. In doing so, we're yielding or availing ourselves to His powerful work.

Of course Paul isn't telling us to abandon all else for the sake of prayer, but to incorporate prayer throughout our daily routine. Because various circumstances call for diverse forms of communication, Ephesians 6:18 also instructs us to pray on all occasions with all kinds of prayer requests. For example, we are daily presented with opportunities to acknowledge the Lord through prayers of praise (Psalm 34:1). Genuine praise is a result of choosing to allow our senses to acknowledge God.

Are you reminded of God's kindness when you experience a cool breeze on a hot summer day? Do you praise God for His continuous faithfulness as you purchase your weekly groceries? Is it your habit to celebrate God's sovereignty in the circumstances of life? By communicating with God through praise, we focus on the truth of His nature and our need for further reliance on His strength.

In addition to praise, focusing our thoughts and communication on God through thanksgiving prompts us to view things from His perspective (1 Chronicles 16:8–11). Just as praise acknowledges who God is, thanksgiving conveys gratitude for all He does. Acknowledging God through prayers of thanksgiving helps us to consider all God is doing around us. Do you consistently thank God for His provision of a good job, warm bed, hot meal? Are you grateful for His gift of family and friends in your life? Are you thankful that God is always working on your behalf?

Those who trust in Christ's power will not only thank Him for what He's already accomplished, but also for what He is going to do. There may be occasions when urgency creates a need to cry out to the Lord for immediate help. If we're consistently focused on God's nature and aware of His constant presence, we'll maintain a thankful heart. There's enormous comfort in knowing that Almighty God is constantly on call and ready to meet our every need.

Have you ever considered the fact that everything we need, God is? Yet sometimes our needs go unmet because we fail to ask God or depend on Him (James 4:2). Rather than becoming discouraged, anxious, or disappointed, we can pause to consider our immediate need. Does the situation require supernatural patience or perseverance? Are you in need of perfect wisdom? Develop the habit of asking God to meet each specific need and rely on His supernatural power to do so.

In discipling others, show them that the Bible tells us that Jesus regularly allotted time to be quiet in prayer before God the Father (Luke 5:16). Following His example, we, too, should create uninterrupted time with God, free from noise and distractions. Encourage each person to ask the Lord to show them quiet moments to spend with Him in prayer. Then, be careful not to fill that time with other activities.

Remind others that God has purpose in all things and that each moment of our lives has potential for spiritual significance. Encourage them to remain in Jesus by engaging in continuous dialogue with Him throughout the day. Ask them to think about occasions when they've spent an entire day with a close friend. Show them that they didn't stop what they were doing to talk to one another, but incorporated conversation into each activity in which they participated. The same should be true of our relationship with Jesus; the difference is that He is always with us.

Also, teach them that Jesus is our ever-present source of help (Psalm 46:1). Train them to convert each need into a prayer request, and to rely on the Lord's strength to meet each and every need. Through learning to pray in every circumstance, those you mentor will grow in their reliance on the power of God and anticipate His eternal purpose being achieved in their lives.

CHAPTER SEVENTEEN

How to Study the Bible for Application

We've learned that each of us can experience Christ's victory through the personal practice of biblical principles. To put it simply, Scripture is the tool and application is the means used to achieve obedience. Therefore, each time we read, study, meditate on, and memorize God's Word it should ultimately be for the purpose of personal application. The following practices will help you learn to use the Bible as a tool for implementing truth in your daily routine. Remember, learning to walk in truth is a process that takes practice—the more truth that's applied in your daily life, the greater and more thorough the transforming work.

Begin by choosing a place to study the Bible that's free from noise and distractions. Before starting to read, ask the Holy Spirit to help you understand what is read (Colossians 1:9–10). As you study Scripture from a teachable position, there will be times when the Spirit will prompt you to think or act in a new way. When this happens, rather than continuing to read, stop to allow the Lord to fully reveal His will to you. Then, respond in obedience by immediately putting it into practice.

If—Then

When we study the Bible, we can learn to distinguish God's perspective from a worldview. This knowledge provides us with a choice of whether or not to obey His will. It's a simple, yet significant, fact that God promises to bless our obedience. Let's practice identifying in Scripture God's specific desired action for obedience and the blessing that will result, by reading Deuteronomy 11:26–28: *See, I am setting before you today a blessing and a curse—the blessing if you obey the commands of the LORD your God that I am giving you today; the curse if you disobey the commands of the LORD your God and turn from the way I command you today by following other gods, which you have not known.* Here, God associates the blessings of obedience with personal choice.

Proverbs 2:1–6 says, *My son, if you accept my words and store up my commands within you, turning your ear to wisdom and applying your heart to understanding, and if you call out for insight and cry aloud for understanding, and if you look for it as for silver and search for it as for hidden treasure, then you will understand the fear of the LORD and find the knowledge of God. For the LORD gives wisdom, and from his mouth come knowledge and understanding.*

From these verses, we can identify desired acts of obedience and the expected blessing by noting the words *if* and *then*. *If* denotes a potential choice and *then* signifies a potential consequence. If we obey God's Word, then the result is God's blessings. If we disobey His Word, then the eventual consequence will be unpleasant. The stipulation of obedience preceding God's blessing is consistent throughout Scripture and is key in evaluating correct application of truth.

By using the "if—then" method of application, even though the words *if* and *then* may not appear in a verse, we can identify obedience and disobedience. For instance, Matthew 6:33 says, *But seek first his kingdom and his righteousness, and all these things will be given to you as well.* Using this verse, let's practice considering what obedience looks like by identifying both the promise and the stipulation to the promise. *If* we strive to seek God first in every area of life by pursuing righteousness (stipulation), *then* we can confidently expect the Lord to provide everything we need (promised blessing). However, we shouldn't expect God to provide for our well-being *if* we fail to give Christ first place in our hearts and lives. The promise of blessing only holds true when the truth is applied correctly.

We can also learn to distinguish obedience from disobedience by separating the choices that mirror God's Word from those that reflect the world. For example, in Galatians 5:16 Paul wrote, *So I say, live by the Spirit, and you will not gratify the desires of the sinful nature.* We correctly apply the principle in this verse *if* we choose to live under the control of the Holy Spirit. *Then* we will please God by not pursuing our selfish desires. Conversely, *if* we choose to pursue our sinful nature, *then* we're not living by the Spirit or pleasing God.

As you can see, learning to distinguish God's will from those things that oppose it makes the choice to walk in obedience clearer. Although this method of application is effective for walking in truth, it will take practice to develop these habits as a way of life. Be diligent, yet patient in the process of daily applying God's Word in your heart and life, trusting God to bless your efforts.

In discipling others, it's beneficial to use words and transitional phrases to help move a person from knowledge and understanding of truth to application of it, resulting in obedience and blessing. Using this method of study, the words and phrases might look like this: *if* the Bible teaches this, *then* it reflects God's best for you. *If* God says it, *then* you should believe and obey it, trusting He will bless your obedience. Encourage others to rely on insight provided by the Lord to best determine personal application and to walk by faith in what He shows them to do.

Teaching, Rebuking, Correcting, Training

Let's examine another method of studying Scripture for application by using 2 Timothy 3:16: *All Scripture is God-breathed and is useful for* teaching, rebuking, correcting *and* training *in righteousness.* [Emphasis added.] This verse shows God's Word to be applicable for every situation and circumstance. Therefore, when reading the Bible, it's valuable to consider what God may want us to specifically comprehend and put into practice.

Using the subjects highlighted in the above verse will help us to do just that. For example, while reading the Bible for content, ask the Holy Spirit to provide personal understanding and application by using the following questions: Is this Scripture *teaching* a specific truth? If so, what is that truth and how does it apply to your life? Does it represent a *rebuke* or criticism of your actions? If so, God wants you to ask for forgiveness and rely on Him to help you change the behavior. Does this verse provide instruction in *correcting* undesired behavior? If so, immediately respond by obeying what is revealed. Is this Scripture bringing to light a new spiritual discipline for your life? Is it trying to *train* you in implementing a skill that would promote righteousness? If so, consistently practice its principles.

We can practice this method for applying truth by turning to the Book of Jonah, found in the Old Testament. Begin reading Jonah 1:1: *The word of the LORD came to Jonah son of Amittai.* Then, keeping in mind the aforementioned subjects and questions, ask God to show you what He wants you to do in response to what you've read. For instance, Jonah 1:1 reveals that God is all-knowing and personal, coming very specifically, directly, and personally to Jonah the son of Amittai. Could it be that God wants to teach you to recognize His presence in your life? Perhaps He wants you to grasp how much He cares about the details throughout your day. This verse also reveals that the Lord spoke to Jonah. Perhaps God wants you to see His desire to speak into your life, or train you to become increasingly intentional in developing your relationship with Him.

Let's practice this method again using Jonah 1:2: *"Go to the great city of Nineveh and preach against it, because its wickedness has come up before me."* Here God is teaching Jonah what He wants him to do. He's also training Jonah to stretch his faith by asking him to leave those things that are most familiar and comfortable in order to fulfill God's will. How could these truths currently apply in your life? Is God calling you to perform a specific task on His behalf? Is He asking you to boldly communicate truth to others? Could He be leading you to move in a direction that is unfamiliar in order to further His kingdom?

Are you recognizing the numerous potential life applications from a single verse of Scripture? Because God wants to do a thorough, transforming work in our lives, it's of great benefit to slow down and allow His Word and Spirit to teach, rebuke, correct, and train us in righteousness.

In discipling others, encourage them to practice this method of Bible application, being careful to avoid becoming distracted by the verse assessment process. More important than trying to decide whether or not a verse represents teaching, rebuking, correcting, or training are the lessons learned. These four categories should merely serve as a means to begin thinking about practical application for their lives.

Since every spiritual journey is unique, help others to realize that the lessons God may want to teach them may differ from those He is teaching others. Also, the same verse God uses to present application in their life today may reveal different application in the future. Remind those you mentor that God makes His Word applicable, so we'll practice its principles and experience victory in each circumstance we face.

Chapter and Verse

We continually want to keep in mind that application of truth is the primary goal of Bible study. This means that even though you may be studying a large section of Scripture, you'll want to learn to break the passage into smaller groupings of verses to more easily recognize possible applications. When studying the Bible, particularly in this fashion, it can be valuable to first consider the individual book's author, the time and surrounding circumstances in which it was written, and who the book was written to or about. This information will assist you in studying Scripture in its correct context and is included in many Bibles at the beginning of each book.

As you begin reading a chapter from the Bible, think about the overall subject or theme of the chapter and write it on a piece of paper. Then, consider how the chapter could be divided into smaller sections or groups of verses by identifying a change in thought or direction. Distinguish each section by providing a short theme that describes the general subject matter it contains. Then, write each theme with its corresponding verses under the original chapter theme.

Further examine these smaller sections of verses individually by relying on the Holy Spirit for insight into personal application. Using either statements or questions, write out what the Spirit reveals to you.

Then, put into practice what you've learned. This may seem like a lot to do in order to study a chapter. But since our ultimate goal is application, we'll need to find specific principles within a larger context in order to implement them in our lives.

To help us practice this method of study, let's use the first chapter of the Book of Jonah as our example. (Reexamining this passage of Scripture will show the difference between this study method and the previous one.) Remember, since personal application of the same Scripture passage may differ from one person to another, the outline God provides you may be different from the one below.

Begin by reading the entire first chapter of Jonah, verses 1–17. Now consider the chapter's overall subject matter or theme. Since this is Jonah's introduction in Scripture, I entitled the overall theme "Jonah's Journey Begins." Next, read the chapter again to divide it into sections and identify each section using a theme to describe its specific subject matter. (These divisions may be distinguishable by a change in thought or direction.) Write each theme with its corresponding verses under the overall chapter theme. As you continue to be sensitive to the Holy Spirit, write out pertinent applications for each section using either statements or questions.

In discipling others, advise them that this method is particularly helpful for visual learners who benefit from writing out thoughts and seeing steps presented on paper and also for those who like to grasp an overall picture prior to examining details. Even though the person you're mentoring may study a large passage of Scripture at one time, encourage them to take the necessary steps to apply each individual lesson within the passage.

Jonah Chapter 1: Jonah's Journey Begins
(Overall Subject Matter/Theme)

Jonah 1:1–3 Jonah Tries to Flee from the Lord (Section Theme)

- What are my typical reactions when God reveals His will to me? In what ways do I try to run from the Lord?
- Since my actions reveal my heart motive, I should invite the Lord to consistently evaluate my heart motive.

Jonah 1:4–7 Jonah's Rebellion Results in Distress (Section Theme)

- What do my actions say to others concerning my relationship with God?
- My individual choices can and often do affect others. Therefore, I should choose to act under the authority of Christ.

Jonah 1:8–14 Challenging Circumstances Lead to Questions (Section Theme)

- In what ways might God use trying times to prompt me to consider my spiritual condition?
- The Lord will use the lives of those around me to point me back to Him. God uses the suffering of consequences to move me to repentance.

Jonah 1:15–16 Jonah's Disobedience Results in Undesired Consequences (Section Theme)

- What is my typical response when I recognize disobedience in my life?
- When I choose to disobey, I miss the opportunity to honor God. When I recognize disobedience in my life, my response should be immediate repentance.

Jonah 1:17 God Is Eternally Faithful (Section Theme)

- Do I easily recognize and acknowledge God's supernatural provision in my life?
- Even when I fail, the Lord is faithful. God's provision is unlimited. God will orchestrate circumstances to encourage me to stop and prompt me to think.

From experience, some people prefer application through the use of statements rather than questions, or vice versa. Sharing this insight with those you disciple should free them to use whichever means best facilitates personal application. Teach each person to practice a variety of methods of studying the Bible for application. Then, encourage them to use those methods that are most beneficial to their individual learning style and spiritual development.

Personal Identification

Another way to effectively study the Bible for application is to intentionally identify with the Scripture you're reading, in much the same way you identify with things common to life. For example, I watch the national news to gain knowledge. At times I'm moved by a particular story because I can identify with the circumstances or characters involved. Perhaps a family reminds me of my own, or the issues facing a community or local government are similar to mine. As I identify with the choices made or the consequences suffered, I can be influenced to change the way I think or behave. Similarly, by identifying with the characters and situations in the Bible I can be influenced to apply truth, resulting in meaningful life changes.

Let's practice this method of study using Jonah 2:1: *From inside the fish Jonah prayed to the LORD his God.* To identify with a character or situation in the Bible, ask yourself questions to consider how you might relate to what's happening. For instance, after reading Jonah 2:1, consider what you might be thinking and feeling as if you were Jonah. Perhaps you would be wondering, in horror, how you got into this predicament. Would you be pondering ways to get out? Would you be frightened, lonely, or discouraged?

Next, ask the Lord to reveal the lessons He wants you to learn from Jonah's example.

- For instance, as with Jonah, sometimes the difficult situations we find ourselves in are a result of our disobedience to God. Therefore, to avoid the suffering of unnecessary consequences, we should learn to walk in immediate obedience to Him.

- By confining him to the inside of the fish, God put Jonah in a position to be still. How sad it is when God has to use such drastic measures to gain the attention of His children. Because God always desires His best for us, it would benefit us to choose to be still before Him in prayer, inviting Him to align our will with His rather than pursuing our own way.

- Through the severity of Jonah's predicament, he finally came to the end of himself and realized his need for God. Sometimes the Lord will allow us to experience increasingly adverse consequences to prompt us to recognize our lack of reliance on Him.

- Jonah acknowledged God as his true source of help by crying out in prayer. We, too, should remember that no matter how grim things appear, it's never too late to turn to God.

There are often numerous lessons that can be learned from a single verse of Scripture through the method of personal identification. This can be further practiced through the study of both characters and circumstances in the Old and New Testaments of the Bible.

In discipling others, remind them that God provided His Word of instruction so we might avoid personal error by learning from the choices and consequences of others. As we identify with each biblical example, we can learn what is and is not pleasing to the Lord and apply these lessons in our own lives.

Topical Study

Sometimes people want to study a specific subject in the Bible. Since our goal is to become doers rather than merely hearers of God's Word, it's essential to transition from knowledge of a particular subject to application of it. This means that we should first study a subject to gain biblical knowledge. Then, we can pursue practical understanding in order to implement its principles.

Let's consider, for example, the subject of patience. What does the Bible have to say about patience? What are the qualities of someone who is patient? What steps do I need to take to become patient? Notice the significance of the order of the previous questions. The first question considers knowledge of the subject being studied; the next question points to practical understanding; and the final question points to personal application.

What if the subject being studied is a place? Let's consider the town of Bethlehem. What are some questions we could ask to help us move from mere knowledge of this town to personal application? Where is Bethlehem located and why was it significant in Scripture? Who were some of the people who lived there? What role did Bethlehem play in the lives of Christ-followers? Remember, after studying pertinent Scripture for knowledge and understanding, ask God to provide you with personal application: Why should I consider Bethlehem's importance today, and how does it pertain to me?

Sometimes the subject of inquiry may be a person. Let's use the example of a high priest and consider his significance in Scripture and application for us today. For example, what does it mean for someone to be referred to as a high priest in the Bible? How was a high priest appointed? Is there a difference between a high priest in the Old and New Testaments? As a follower of Jesus, how should this knowledge influence me? Remember, without application there is no change. Therefore, topical studies should also result in personal application.

You may find it valuable to use a Bible concordance when researching topics of interest. (A concordance is an alphabetical index of subjects in the Bible. Although these are included in the back of many modern Bibles, separately published concordances provide more exhaustive word searches as well as Hebrew and Greek lexicons.) Even though a concordance may prove helpful when studying subjects in the Bible, there are times when a topic is not specifically mentioned in Scripture. In these instances, it is necessary to examine a topic in the Bible from a broader perspective.

For example, let's presume someone asks you what specific words the Bible considers to be profanity. Using a Bible concordance, we find specific Scripture references for the words *profane* and *cursing*. After studying these references, we realize that none of them pertain to specific words that would be considered profanity. However, if we were to broaden our search to include related topics such as *speech*, *word*, and *talk* we would find verses that apply in both a specific and broader sense. Consider Ephesians 4:29, for example: *Do not let any unwholesome talk come out of your mouths, but only what is helpful for building others up according to their needs, that it may benefit those who listen.* Ephesians 5:4 teaches that we shouldn't use obscenity, foolish talk, or coarse joking. We can conclude that instead of merely drawing a line at profanity, we should examine all our speech to determine whether it is pleasing to God.

When studying the Bible for subject content, you'll find some verses to be precise in their meaning and with specific applications. Philippians 2:14, for instance, says, *Do everything without complaining or arguing.* To apply this verse we should evaluate our behavior to see that in each area of our lives we are choosing to abstain from arguing and complaining.

This doesn't mean that we'll always agree on every issue or that we shouldn't voice genuine concerns. It means that we should conscientiously communicate and discuss matters in a manner that pleases Christ.

Even though Bible passages should be considered in their appropriate context, some Scripture could also be applied to other areas of living. We find such a verse in 2 Corinthians 9:8: *And God is able to make all grace abound to you, so that in all things at all times, having all that you need, you will abound in every good work.* This promise is written in the context of giving and being able to give as God provides. But, since God's grace is abundantly sufficient, this verse could apply to many other areas of life as well.

We should also realize that, at times, it may be necessary to consider several verses of a particular Bible passage to grasp the correct context and meaning of a word or phrase taken from that text. For example, in 1 Timothy 2:9 Paul wrote, *I also want women to dress modestly, with decency and propriety, not with braided hair or gold or pearls or expensive clothes.* Verse 10 reflects Paul's complete thought, *but with good deeds, appropriate for women who profess to worship God.* If we were to read only verse 9, we might conclude that it's wrong for a woman to braid her hair or wear a strand of pearls. However, the full context reveals that Paul was merely teaching women that their outward appearance and behavior should reflect their inward preparation for genuine worship.

In discipling others, show them how to practice progressing from merely having biblical knowledge of a particular subject, to understanding and practical life application. Then, encourage them to rely on the power of the Holy Spirit to help implement personal change.

Additional Bible Study Tools

As you delve deeper into the truths of God's Word, you may find it helpful to use other Bible-based resources such as commentaries and handbooks. However, rather than quickly turning to additional study aids, choose first to rely primarily on the Holy Spirit to provide you with wisdom, insight, and application of Scripture (1 Corinthians 2:11–12). Also, Bible resources should be checked for accuracy and integrity prior to use. Since God expects each believer to apply Scripture in their own life, we are each responsible to gain personal knowledge and comprehension of the Bible. For this reason, we shouldn't assume that what someone else says is true, but instead diligently learn truth for ourselves (Acts 17:11; 2 Timothy 2:15).

In discipling others, be aware that some people may not be familiar with individual books of the Bible or their location. In these cases, teach them to use the Bible's table of contents. Or, you may want to encourage them to invest in inexpensive tabs to easily flag each book in the Bible. These allow a person to distinguish the beginning of each book for easy access and can be found at most Christian bookstores.

In addition, train those you disicple to carefully choose Bible resources from writers and publishers that are well-established and are well-recognized as proven, accurate authorities in their use and explanation of Scripture. Teach them that thorough application of God's Word is rarely quick or easy, but instead an ongoing and steady process. Encourage them to continually focus on the blessings of walking in obedience to biblical truth rather than on the time and effort it takes to do so.

CHAPTER EIGHTEEN

Applying Truth to Develop Identity in Christ

Since the Bible defines a genuine disciple of Jesus, it serves to reason that it is God's Word, rather than the world, that determines our identity in Him. In this chapter, we'll examine who we are in Christ and learn ways to apply God's truth, thereby developing our true identity in Jesus. Let's begin by looking at 2 Corinthians 5:16–17: *So from now on we regard no one from a worldly point of view. Though we once regarded Christ in this way, we do so no longer. Therefore, if anyone is in Christ, he is a new creation; the old has gone, the new has come!*

Being in Christ affords us access to the powerful work of His Spirit so His unique godly characteristics can be developed within us. As a result, we should no longer view our lives from a human perspective, but from the completed work we can become as we allow Christ's nature to govern us. Did you catch that significant truth? Learning to walk in our true nature in Christ begins with the way we view ourselves.

The Bible teaches that one of the greatest ways to live confidently in Jesus is by consistently viewing our lives from His perspective. This occurs as we continually renew our minds with truth, rather than invest in thoughts of the flesh, and as we allow God's truth to have the final authority. As you can imagine, investing in even the smallest thoughts that oppose our nature in Christ will hinder us from reaching our full potential. Learning and putting into practice the following methods of applying truth will help you develop your genuine identity in Jesus.

Exchanging Lies for Truth

For many people the "old self"' has developed thought patterns, habits, and behaviors over the years that may be considered acceptable by the world's standards, but are in opposition to their new life in Christ. Some people have accepted thoughts about themselves or labels placed on them by others that in no way reflect God's view of them. These old patterns won't diminish on their own or as a result of self-effort (Romans 7:18). Instead, they must be surrendered to Jesus in exchange for His truth in order to develop the "new self" that reflects His nature.

Paul explained this process in Ephesians 4:22–24: *You were taught, with regard to your former way of life, to put off your old self, which is being corrupted by its deceitful desires; to be made new in the attitude of your minds; and to put on the new self, created to be like God in true righteousness and holiness.* Again we see that experiencing our true identity in Christ begins with our mind-set (vs. 23).

Interesting, isn't it? Walking by faith will always begin with a mind-set—a mind set on truth. We then activate the faith God provides to us by believing and trusting in truth. Therefore, living by faith concerning our identity in Jesus cannot be based on what we think of ourselves or what others say about us. It must be based on what God says.

Let's practice recognizing and exchanging ideas that oppose our identity in Christ Jesus by using some examples from real life. Perhaps you have experienced thoughts or feelings such as these: "I'm not as smart as others," "I'm not talented enough to succeed," or "I'll never be good enough". If we buy into this way of thinking, it can lead to a lifetime of discouragement, acceptance of ridicule by others, or a lack of confidence. However, the good news is that these thoughts and feelings in no way represent the true identity of a child of God. Therefore, they need to be removed and exchanged for thoughts that do.

Psalm 139:13 tells us, *For you created my inmost being; you knit me together in my mother's womb.* Imagine this: Before anyone ever met you, our loving God was painstakingly creating you, attentive to every detail. God intentionally designed you exactly as He desires you to be with everything necessary to fulfill His purpose for your life. In choosing to lay down the lies of inadequacy for the truth of God's created identity, we exchange disappointment for the promise of God's designed purpose being fulfilled.

Please don't misunderstand, the thoughts and feelings that we experience are very real. But what if they fail to mirror truth? By aligning our thoughts with God's perspective, our true identity is revealed. For example, perhaps you've made decisions or hesitated to make decisions based on fear—fear of someone's opinion of you, fear of not pleasing others, or fear of not meeting expectations. Even though feelings of fear are real, the source of fear isn't God (Isaiah 41:13). Therefore, human fear neither reflects Christ's nature nor your nature in Him. As you can see, revelation of truth shines the light of God's perspective on our lives, revealing the choice to walk in our true identity in Jesus.

Begin today considering any thoughts and feelings you have about yourself that are contrary to God's perspective, and then practice exchanging each one for truth. By consistently laying down thoughts and feelings that fail to reflect truth to walk in those that do, you'll grow ever stronger in the nature Christ has given you.

In discipling others, help them to see that experiencing their created identity in Jesus begins with a mind set on truth. Encourage them to practice renewing their mind with the truth of Jesus' nature and trusting in His Spirit to develop Christ's characteristics in them. Remind them that the Lord is always available and willing to work to create transformation in their lives. However, our loving God will never force such change. We must surrender to allow Him to do His work.

Truth Is Therefore

We've learned that dividing out ideas that reflect the world from those that mirror truth enables us to distinguish thoughts and behaviors that will most identify us with Christ. Let's now practice these precepts while also using the phrase *truth is* and the word *therefore* to transition from identifying thoughts and feelings to personal application of truth. Let's presume, for example, that you experience thoughts of incompetence, or feelings of being a failure. The *truth is* that God is perfect and, *therefore*, didn't make mistakes in creating us. The *truth is* that even though we're each limited in our human condition, God's power is made perfect in our weaknesses (2 Corinthians 12:9). *Therefore*, we can trust God to achieve His will regardless of human shortcomings.

The *truth is* that each of us is of great worth to Jesus, demonstrated by the enormous price He paid for our lives. *Therefore*, we should accept the value God places on our lives. When we're confronted with negative or self-deprecating thoughts, we should lay them down, exchanging them for truth. Even though developing this method of application will take practice, be encouraged by the significant difference it will make to walk in your true identity!

In discipling others, remind them that the quicker they arrive at truth, the more likely they are to avoid deception. Encourage them to practice using the phrase *truth is* to immediately help them identify and focus on God's perspective in each and every situation. As a result of identifying biblical truth, they can then use the word *therefore* to assist in considering appropriate application and then, rely on the Lord to experience His nature at work within them.

Temporal vs. Eternal

Yet another tool to help us recognize Christ's nature in us is learning to distinguish tangible qualities from intangible ones—temporal from eternal. The world associates a person's identity with qualities that are tangible—those things that you can see and touch. For example, the world would lead us to believe that success is relative to such things as the amount of money you have, the number of awards you receive, the type of car you drive, your occupation, or the house you live in.

If a person were to invest in this way of thinking, their self-worth would depend on these material things. So what would happen if they were to lose their financial investments or personal and professional achievements? Because their identity was wrapped up in these tangibles, sadly, their identity would also be lost, resulting in insecurity. On the other hand, the qualities God develops within a believer are intangible. They are eternal rather than temporal. When a person invests their life in developing the intangible qualities of God such as joy, patience, kindness, love, peace, and mercy, these qualities can never be taken away from them regardless of circumstances.

In discipling others, you may want to read together 1 Samuel 16:7. This passage shows that man judges by outward appearances, while God looks at the heart. For this reason, encourage others to practice focusing on eternal, rather than temporal, qualities and to invest in developing intangible Christlike qualities. In doing so, they will possess characteristics that last forever.

Identifying with Christ's Attributes

So far in this chapter, we've been looking at ways to lay down old thoughts and feelings in exchange for the truth of our identity in Christ. While it's important to correct any thoughts and feelings that oppose our true nature in Jesus, it's also significant to become proactive in firmly establishing our identity in Him. The following exercise is helpful in understanding Christ's attributes and how they're intended to influence our daily lives.

Begin by writing each letter of the alphabet in a column on the left hand side of a piece of paper. Then, next to each letter write an attribute of God that corresponds to that letter. For example, next to the letter A you might write words such as *all-knowing, almighty, author of all, approachable*, and *always near.* Next to the letter B you may write the words *Bread of life, beautiful*, and *Best Friend.* Next to the letter C you might write *Creator, caring, consuming fire, compassionate, Counselor*, and *Comforter.*

Continue this process until you've created an exhaustive list of as many attributes of Christ as you can. (You may want to use a Bible concordance to assist you in this endeavor.) Don't be concerned that each letter has a corresponding attribute, or that some letters have fewer or more attributes than others. This exercise is merely a tool to develop in you the habit of considering the many characteristics of God and how knowing them can influence your life.

When the list is completed, go back over the list of attributes one by one with the purpose of learning their meaning. For example, the first attribute of God we listed was all-knowing. Truly think about what it means that God is all-knowing. What an amazing God! He knew what time the sun would rise over your house this morning and what exact fraction of the moon will be shining in your window tonight. He is fully aware of the places you go and the routes you take to get there. Psalm 139:1–4 says, *O LORD, you have searched me and you know me. You know when I sit and when I rise; you perceive my thoughts from afar. You discern my going out and my lying down; you are familiar with all my ways. Before a word is on my tongue you know it completely, O LORD.* The fact that God is all-knowing is an incredible truth. But what difference could knowing this truth make in our lives?

Time out. Did you catch the significance of that last question? When you stop to ponder the difference a particular biblical principle could make in your personal life, you're considering the change that should result from practicing its truth. Because truth carries with it the potential to transform lives, by practicing its principles you are training yourself in godliness.

So what difference should the fact that God is all-knowing make in our lives? Because God has full knowledge concerning all things, this truth should influence us to rely on His perfect perspective of our circumstances rather than on our narrow points of view. It should prompt us to seek His wisdom for making decisions instead of relying on the opinions of others. Since nothing is hidden from the Lord, we should strive to make even our most private thoughts and actions pleasing to Him. By doing so, we utilize the knowledge and understanding of this truth in the application of it.

Let's return to our exercise and examine another attribute together. The next attribute listed is almighty. What does it mean that God is almighty? Think about it. God's might doesn't come in small quantities that can be contained in a package; it's unlimited and supernatural. Job 11:7 asks this question: *Can you probe the limits of the Almighty?* It is nearly impossible to fathom the might necessary to create the universe, part the Red Sea, or raise Lazarus to life. Yet God does exercise His might and desires to demonstrate His almighty power in our lives today. What difference should knowledge of this truth make in our lives?

Since the Spirit of God indwells me, His unlimited might is continually available to me. Rather than attempt to limit God with my thoughts, I can choose to rely on His unlimited ability to work mightily in me. Rather than speak of the potential impossibilities, I can choose to place my trust in our unlimited, Almighty God to make a way for me—even in difficult situations. Notice the use of the word choose in describing the difference that recognizing God as almighty can make in my life. What difference will you allow the truth of Christ's attributes to make in your daily life? In what specific ways are you choosing to develop your identity in Him?

As you can imagine, this exercise could take some time to complete. Rather than focus on finishing it, invite the Lord to help you grow in your knowledge of Him and your relationship to Him in the process. Choose to set this book aside for a while, if necessary, to allow God to further develop His nature in you.

In discipling others, it may be necessary to assist them in creating a list of attributes, as well as help in considering their meaning and application. Because this exercise can be life changing, encourage those you disciple to take as long as necessary to complete it. Train them to anticipate seeing and identifying God's attributes at work throughout each day and also to practice relying on His eternal qualities. Let them know that their confidence in Christ will grow as they become increasingly dependent on Him.

CHAPTER NINETEEN

Applying Truth to Fulfill God's Purpose

At one time or another in their lifetime, people will ponder their purpose for living. Do you know why you were created? Are you certain of the purpose for your life? Colossians 1:16 says, *For by him all things were created: things in heaven and on earth, visible and invisible, whether thrones or powers or rulers or authorities; all things were created by him and for him.* It is wonderful to know that even though we are all uniquely created, the Lord purposefully created each of us to live for Him.

As we live and grow in an intimate relationship with the Lord, we experience the Holy Spirit's work in us, our lives are increasingly transformed to mirror Him, and Christ is honored. In addition, God will enable us to train others to faithfully follow Jesus. Now that's a purpose-filled life!

Apart from a personal relationship with Jesus, life can seem empty and meaningless. On the other hand, knowing that we were created as a result of specific design and with intentional purpose brings enormous meaning to living. Acts 17:26–27 provides an example of God's intentionality in creating us: *"From one man he made every nation of men, that they should inhabit the whole earth; and he determined the times set for them and the exact places where they should live. God did this so that men would seek him and perhaps reach out for him and find him, though he is not far from each one of us."* Have you ever wondered why you were born at a particular time or place? Have you considered that your family placement, including your birth order, was appointed by God?

Once again, we can see the significance in examining our lives from God's perspective. In doing so, we're training ourselves to focus on His purpose rather than our own goals and desires, enabling us to better recognize His will and surrender to it. Consequently, we will fulfill His purpose by drawing closer to Christ and bringing honor and glory to His name.

Purpose as a Priority

Fulfilling God's purpose becomes a personal priority when it remains our focus regardless of the situation, the way we're feeling, or the people involved. Let's consider the role of our mind-set in daily living. In Matthew 6:25–32, Jesus instructed His followers to eliminate worry from their lives by choosing to trust in Him. While trusting in Jesus draws us closer to Him and serves to fulfill God's purposes, worry distracts us from it. Think about it: When our focus is on self, circumstances, or what might please others, it's difficult to consider God's perspective or potential purpose. In viewing a situation apart from God's perspective we are excluding truth from our thought process, resulting in increased anxiety or worry. Therefore, worry is the result of misplaced focus.

On the other hand, when our mind-set is on God's perspective and potential purpose in a situation, our focus is on truth. As a result, we are nurturing our faith by being mindful to trust in God's control over the issue, as well as in His power to work on our behalf. This will produce peace and fend off worry. Living through challenging circumstances, while free of worry, reflects victory that only God can provide. Consequently, we experience His blessing, God receives the glory, and His purpose is fulfilled.

In discipling others, help them see that since God is perfect, His purposeful plan for their lives is also perfect. Teach them that making God's purposes a personal priority begins with a mind set on His perspective. Through an understanding and embracing of life's purposes, a disciple can truly fulfill God's will and experience abundant life.

"Get to" vs. "Have To"

In Colossians 3:2, we are instructed to fix our focus on God's perspective and purpose: *Set your minds on things above, not on earthly things.* Although it's easy to allow our minds to be focused on the activities of earth, God desires for us to have our minds set on the eternal things of His kingdom. For this reason, we should develop the habit of considering our focus during the activity of each day. The following exercise will help us learn to do just that.

Think for a moment about the various activities that are a part of your daily life. These may include such things as responsibilities, appointments, recreation, and entertainment. Using a piece of paper, list each activity under the category heading of "Get to Do" or "Have to Do," based on your view of each activity. In other words, is the activity one you look forward to being involved in, or is it something you perceive as an obligation or something you dread? Then, next to each entry, explain your reason for placing that activity under its particular heading. An example is provided below.

Get to Do	(Explanation of Activity)	**Have to Do**	(Explanation of Activity)
Son's Soccer Practice	Satisfaction in watching my child compete.	Dishes/ Laundry	I do not enjoy either of these chores.
Exercise	I enjoy working out and staying fit.	Going to the Dentist	I dislike having someone work on my teeth.
Work	I like getting a paycheck.	Work	I don't particularly enjoy my job.

Remember, in order to consider God's purpose, we must learn to view our lives from His perspective. For example, the world promotes a focus on the benefits to self. Therefore, if an activity fails to provide gratification or isn't convenient, it may be viewed as a "have to," or an obligation. If an activity does provide satisfaction, it may be considered a "get to." This causes me to wonder: Since God has purpose in all things, should a person's focus be dependent on the activity or on the potential purpose of it? Does focus really make a difference?

To answer these questions, let's use the activities listed above to consider God's perspective and potential purpose. In the first example, the person dislikes washing dishes and doing laundry. For many people these chores are seemingly endless tasks requiring continuous effort, and at times involve cleaning up after others. Although these statements are true, might there be potential purpose in such seemingly mundane tasks?

What would it look like to focus our thoughts and energy on fulfilling God's purpose rather than on merely performing each task? We might begin by thinking about the specific people these items represent. As a result, the tasks of washing dishes and doing laundry could become a precious time of praying for these individuals, thanking God for their placement in our lives, and asking the Lord to allow our service to minister to them as we meet their personal needs. By doing so, a task that was once a begrudging "have to" could become a privilege, and God would be honored in the process.

From the previous list, let's also consider the example of going to the dentist. This person dreads their appointment and views the activity as a definite "have to." After all, it's one more obligation in an already hectic day. They don't like the idea of not knowing how long the visit will last, what potential problems might be discovered, and the possible pain and cost that may result. These are certainly valid concerns that are shared by many. But where is their focus?

By changing our focus to the things of God and His potential purpose, our mind-set is on the eternal rather than the temporal. So, instead of viewing the dental appointment as an obligation, they can begin to see it as a potential opportunity to represent Christ in that place. Rather than merely enduring the time spent in the waiting room, they can choose to be focused on and anticipating opportunities God may provide to represent Him to others through action and communication. Also, regardless of the diagnosis and expense resulting from the visit, they can focus on trusting God to meet each and every need, thereby giving honor to Him. Recognizing and accepting the invitation to be a part of God's purpose should help change a mind-set from "have to" to "get to."

Keep in mind that God wants our focus to be continually on His purpose regardless of the activity. This means that even though our culture may influence us to be task-oriented, God wants us to be purpose-oriented. For this reason, we should also consider activities from the "get to" list in light of God's perspective. For example, the person cited on the previous list views attending their son's soccer practice as a "get to." They enjoy being a part of their son's activities, watching him develop his talents, and supporting his efforts. They also like socializing with other parents with similar interests.

We may assume that because a person finds pleasure in a particular activity that they would have a positive attitude throughout the activity. Although this may be true, a positive attitude doesn't always translate into a Christ-centered mind-set. Therefore, we must consider the person's focus. If a person's attention is drawn to the personal benefits of an activity, they may be focusing on things other than God's purpose. For instance, if their focus is merely on soccer, they may engage others in dialogue involving the particulars of the game without considering ways to direct the conversation to the things of God.

On the other hand, if their focus is on glorifying God, they may intentionally relate soccer strategies to God's plan for their child's life. In addition, one who is Christ-focused will be mindful of their words and actions toward players, parents, coaches, and referees, recognizing that they have the potential to represent their Savior in that place. Regardless of the activity, one of the greatest ways we can begin to fulfill God's purpose for our lives is to have a spiritual mind-set. By focusing on God's perspective, each activity can become a means for accomplishing His purpose.

In discipling others, advise them that God doesn't provide activity to deter us from discipleship. He creates it as a means for discipleship! Therefore, we should be anticipating God using us throughout the routine tasks of our day to nurture and develop faith in those around us.

Encourage others to consider the Lord's perspective in their daily routine. Help them remember that His purpose is always the same: to develop a deeper relationship with us in order to bring Himself glory. Having a mind set on God's perspective will aid them in considering ways to live out God's purpose, rather than merely completing the task at hand.

You may want to read together Colossians 3:17: *And whatever you do, whether in word or deed, do it all in the name of the Lord Jesus, giving thanks to God the Father through him.* Then, discuss the enormous blessing it is to enter into a relationship with the living God and to have the privilege of serving under His Lordship. Out of an overflow of abundant thanksgiving for all Jesus has done for us should flow a lifetime of gladly pursuing God's purpose for our lives.

What vs. Why

Let's continue to look at ways to consider God's perspective and potential purpose in the moments of our days. Consider this: Which is more significant, *what* you do or *why* you do it? Of course, it's valuable to consider what you do with the time you've been given, but more significant is why you choose to do what you do. Since answers to "why" reflect heart motive, they will either provide human reasoning for what we do, or reveal a heart pursuing God's potential purpose. Therefore, it's valuable for us to learn to evaluate why we do what we do.

To prove this point, let's consider the activity of going to the grocery store: something many people do on a regular basis. What are the reasons we might give for *why* we go to the grocery store? My family needs to eat, we're out of milk, there's a good sale, etc. Even though people could easily identify with these responses, the obvious reasons might not reveal God's potential purpose.

As I ponder God's perspective, my focus turns from the reasons for the task to thinking about the potential purpose in it. In doing so, I view going to the grocery store as an opportunity to honor Jesus by representing Him to those around me—thereby fulfilling my purpose. Because my mind-set is focused on God, what might once be considered inconveniences are now opportunities: showing kindness through assisting an elderly shopper, waiting patiently in the crowded aisles, and conveying mercy to the clerk who unknowingly makes a mistake. Purpose changes everything! Even the long checkout line that was once a personal dread can become an occasion for purposeful conversation. Rather than thinking of all that needs to get done, focusing on God's perspective helps us to be purposeful in all we do!

Consider another example. Let's assume you like to play golf and do so regularly with a group of friends. What would be the reasons you would give for *why* you participate in this activity? Would it be the enjoyment, relaxation, competition, or socialization? But what is your purpose for playing? As with any activity, our purpose is to grow closer to Christ and to honor Him. How you react when you aren't hitting the ball particularly well; how you respond when you take the lead; the topics of conversation you choose; as well as the people you meet in the parking lot, clubhouse, and golf course are all avenues to honor Jesus. Have you ever played golf with purpose? Once you do, you'll realize that the game will never be the same.

So what is the evidence that we are focused on purpose? Believers who choose to focus on God's purpose consistently ask Him to allow them to see circumstances from His perspective. They practice surrendering their own desires to accomplish His purpose. They anticipate His mighty work around them, in them, and through them. Because the number of days we each live here on earth have already been determined by God (Psalm 139:16), those who want to fulfill His will, rather than merely pleasing themselves, will focus on their eternal purpose for living.

In discipling others, teach them that whatever the activity, it's never about the task and always about the purpose. The Bible teaches that disciples of Jesus are the light of the world. In Matthew 5:16 Jesus said, *"Let your light shine before men, that they may see your good deeds and praise your Father in heaven."* Enable others to see that we don't have to create purposeful activity—it is all around us. Everywhere we go there are people who need to see in us the light of Jesus. Instead of allowing all the places we go to represent an associated task, we are to view each activity and the routes in between as avenues created by God to provide opportunities to achieve His purposes.

A Purpose for Every Season

In addition to the purpose that God has in the moments of our days, He also provides purpose in the seasons of life. This means that whatever season you may be experiencing, you can trust that the Lord has specific purpose in it. Sometimes people want to move past a particular season or phase in life rather than embrace the significant purpose it provides. However, throughout the seasons of our lives, God desires to use us for His immediate purpose, prepare us for His future purpose, or sometimes both at the same time.

Consider, for example, the biblical account of Joseph. His life was filled with pain and adversity, but it also included enormous purpose. As a young man, God was working in his life (Genesis 37:5–11). Rejected by his brothers and separated from his father, he learned to rely on God rather than on man (Genesis 37:23–27). In his youth, Joseph was sold into slavery where he lived as a humble servant (Genesis 37:36). God didn't remove Joseph from his difficult circumstances but, instead, gave him favor in them. As a result, he was put in charge of his master's estate (Genesis 39:2–4). Even though Joseph led a life of integrity, he was wrongly accused, imprisoned, and forgotten (Genesis 39:19–20).

As you can imagine, many would consider Joseph's life as one of the most challenging in all of Scripture, yet God had great purpose in it. The personal adversity served God's purpose of drawing Joseph closer to Himself while bringing Him honor in the process (Genesis 39:3, 23; 40:8; 41:16, 38). Remember, God is either using us for His purpose, preparing us for His purpose, or doing both at the same time. God used seasons of hardship in Joseph's life to fulfill His purpose while preparing him for future kingdom work.

Eventually, God placed Joseph as second in command to Pharaoh in Egypt to prevent the people from starving during a famine. When reunited with some of the people who had mistreated him, Joseph said, *"You intended to harm me, but God intended it for good to accomplish what is now being done, the saving of many lives."* (Genesis 50:20). How very precious that, through it all, Joseph continued pursuing God's perspective and purpose.

Take a moment to consider your current circumstances. Are you striving to see your life from God's point of view? Could it be that God wants to use this season in your life to draw you closer to Himself and to bring Him glory? Have you considered the ways God may be using this time to prepare you for future purpose?

In discipling others, teach them that rather than merely enduring or enjoying a particular season of life, God wants them to pursue His potential purpose in it. Use God's Word to help others view situations from the Lord's perspective and to consider His potential purpose in them.

God saved us because of His grace and purpose (2 Timothy 1:9), and we can have confidence that He will continue to work out His salvation in us to His determined completion (Philippians 1:6). This means that even though our lives aren't perfect, they should reflect a spiritual work in progress. Let others know that as we continue to apply truth in our daily lives, we can be confident that He will achieve His will and purpose.

CHAPTER TWENTY

Applying Truth to Correct Sin and Prevent Future Disobedience

The Bible refers to God's truth as light (Psalm 119:105). When a person desires to be Christlike, they want to eliminate the darkness of sin in their life by applying the light of truth. First John 1:5–7 tells us, *This is the message we have heard from him and declare to you: God is light; In him there is no darkness at all. If we claim to have fellowship with him yet walk in darkness, we lie and do not live by the truth. But if we walk in the light, as he is in the light, we have fellowship with one another, and the blood of Jesus, his Son, purifies us from all sin.*

Think about it: When we try to walk across a dark room, we stumble blindly. But when light appears or is introduced in the room, we can see clearly a safe path. Similarly, sin opposes the light of Christ.

Walking in sin blinds us to truth, causes us to stumble, and can have the same effect on others. In the same way light dispels darkness in a room, the light of Christ Jesus dispels darkness in our lives. If we desire to correct personal sin, we will intentionally apply the light of truth to our personal thoughts and actions to determine if they've become darkened by sin. We'll then use the light of truth to direct our path and avoid walking in future disobedience.

Let's look at some ways to apply, or put into practice, God's light of truth concerning the correction and prevention of wrong thinking and doing.

Heart Condition

God is always most interested in the condition of our heart. Therefore, when we become intentional in correcting thoughts and behaviors that offend Him, it only makes sense to acknowledge the symptoms of sin and determine the root cause. What's the difference between a symptom and the root cause? Symptoms are recognizable through inward thoughts and feelings and outward behavior that oppose the nature of Jesus and His Word. But they stem from a deeper root cause: the condition of the heart. In other words, if your thoughts, feelings, or actions fail to mirror Jesus, these are indications, or symptoms, of a deeper spiritual issue that needs to be investigated.

Consider this: If you see a doctor for a chronic cough, do you want him to merely treat the cough or do you expect him to do a more thorough job of finding the source of the cough? Interestingly, when the root cause of the cough is cured, the cough will be cured as well. In a similar way, God desires to do a thorough work in our lives by diagnosing and curing the root cause of the symptoms we experience when we miss the mark of truth.

God's Word will penetrate deep within us to determine and reveal our true heart condition (Hebrews 4:12), concerning any situation or subject (2 Timothy 3:16–17). We can then choose to apply God's truth and rely on His power to correct the heart issue as well as eradicate the symptoms. It's really that simple.

For example, sometimes believers exhibit symptoms such as fear or worry without ever considering the deeper heart issue. In pursuing freedom from such symptoms, let's use the ever-important *why* question to help us examine the root cause. Why do we experience fear and worry? Since we experience these symptoms most often when situations are beyond our control, one heart issue would be our desire for control. The Bible teaches that God is in control of all things. Therefore, we can apply this truth by choosing to trust in His authority, thereby solving our heart issue problem as well as the symptoms of fear and worry.

In addition to asking ourselves why we experience a particular ungodly symptom, we can also consider what truth says about these symptoms to help us diagnose the root heart issue. For example, sometimes people experience thoughts and feelings of being overwhelmed. The truth is, that God will enable us to do everything He asks of us (2 Corinthians 9:8). Therefore, if we become overwhelmed, we either have a heart desirous of doing more than God asks of us or one that is bent toward self-effort rather than reliance on Christ. In choosing to apply this truth, we will rely on God's strength to follow His directives for our lives, thereby curing the heart issue as well as the symptom of being overwhelmed.

Be careful: The enemy finds great pleasure in believers leaving symptoms unresolved that misrepresent Christ. He knows that application of truth enables us to thoroughly correct issues that oppose the heart of God and would result in freedom from sin. If he can convince us to avoid application of truth, personal sin will remain undiagnosed and untreated, becoming more deeply rooted in our hearts and lives.

In discipling others, help them to recognize the difference between spiritual symptoms and more deeply rooted heart issues. Encourage them to become sensitive to even the smallest personal symptoms that miss the mark of righteousness. Train them to rely on God's truth and power to identify and correct the deeper issues of the heart, allowing them to walk in victory over sin.

A Yielded Heart

God desires for our hearts to remain tender, sensitive to the convicting power of the Holy Spirit. Yielding our hearts to the Spirit's correction results in genuine brokenness and remorse over sin rather than indifference to it. Psalm 51:17 tells us, *The sacrifices of God are a broken spirit; a broken and contrite heart, O God, you will not despise.* Although the world avoids brokenness by urging us to justify wrongdoing, God recognizes this heart condition as a sacrifice, an act of obedience unto Him.

As we continually yield our hearts to God, we should expect Him to prompt us to consider any needed changes in action or direction. Sometimes the Holy Spirit will use specific Scripture to convict us, or give us a mental impression to reveal His truth to us. We can recognize an impression as potentially being from God when the thought is not our own and it aligns with God's character and His Word. The Lord will sometimes use godly counsel, circumstances, or consequences to confirm His leading; and, again, He does so in a manner that always reflects His nature and His Word. Is your heart consistently yielded to the promptings, conviction, and correction of the Holy Spirit?

Developing a heart that remains yielded to Christ and His directives takes practice. Begin by consistently placing yourself in a position of humbleness before the Lord. (A heart of humility acknowledges human imperfections while guarding against pride and the reluctance to admit wrong.)

Also, practice becoming increasingly sensitive to the promptings of the Holy Spirit. Isaiah 30:21 tells us, *Whether you turn to the right or to the left, your ears will hear a voice behind you, saying, "This is the way; walk in it."* As a Christ-follower, you can be confident that God will direct and guide you as you yield your heart to Him.

Then, rely on God to enable you to consistently correct undesired behavior. Rest assured that, as you strive to walk in obedience to the Lord, His power will sustain you. Psalm 37:23–24 says, *If the LORD delights in a man's way, he makes his steps firm; though he stumble, he will not fall, for the LORD upholds him with his hand.*

In discipling others, teach them that genuine discipleship is a continuous process of learning to yield their hearts and adapt their lifestyle to fulfill Christ's will. In order to accomplish this, it's necessary that we rely on God's involvement, including correction. Psalm 139:23–24 says, *Search me, O God, and know my heart; test me and know my anxious thoughts. See if there is any offensive way in me, and lead me in the way everlasting.* A heart yielded to righteousness will rely on the Holy Spirit to identify and correct personal sin while learning to avoid future disobedience.

Reactive vs. Proactive

Whether it is considered or not, heart motive is established prior to action. To put it simply: actions reflect heart condition. For this reason, it's important to provide the Holy Spirit with an open invitation to continually evaluate both our heart condition as well as our personal behavior. It's also significant to recognize the difference between these two types of evaluations.

Motive (choice) → Action (choice) → Outcome (purpose)

When God evaluates behavior, it's after an action or series of actions have taken place and is, therefore, *reactive*. Even though we ask God to evaluate personal behavior with the intention of correcting past sin, the completed action and resulting consequences may not be reversible. However, when we allow God to evaluate our heart motive prior to action, we are becoming *proactive* in preventing undesired choices and behavior. Is it your habit to act without thinking about the motive behind your actions?

God's Word continually encourages us to apply truth to correct personal sin (reactive) and to prevent future disobedience (proactive). For example, Proverbs 28:13 says, *He who conceals his sins does not prosper, but whoever confesses and renounces them finds mercy.* Confessing, rather than concealing sin, is the appropriate reaction to personal wrongdoing. In addition, renouncing sin is choosing to be proactive in preventing further disobedience and results in God's blessing of mercy.

Apart from divine revelation, we will naturally trust in ourselves and see our ways as innocent of wrong doing (Proverbs 16:2). Learning to align our motives with those of Christ prior to action, will prevent us from making our own path and will result in blessing rather than regret. Even though the Holy Spirit will prompt us to correct undesired behavior (reactive), He wants us to become increasingly proactive by learning from our mistakes and putting into practice His truth.

In discipling others, help them to grasp the difference between being spiritually reactive and proactive. Encourage them to focus on the benefits of becoming increasingly proactive by allowing Christ to evaluate heart motive prior to action.

You may also want to share with them Hebrews 12:1: *Therefore, since we are surrounded by such a great cloud of witnesses, let us throw off everything that hinders and the sin that so easily entangles, and let us run with perseverance the race marked out for us.* Then, point out the challenge for us to be both reactive and proactive concerning the elimination of personal sin. To avoid being continually reactive, this verse calls us to account for our personal knowledge of truth by throwing off, or consistently ridding our lives of the sin that can so easily trap us. We are then urged to be proactive by choosing to run the race marked out for us by Jesus, which is the course of personal sanctification.

This verse also reminds us that the Christian life is a process and encourages us to persevere in it. Because the person you disciple will continually be exposed to new methods of applying truth, consistently encourage them to stay the course of faith!

Examine Direction and Action

We've discovered that obedience to Christ is determined by direction and action: where you are going and what you are doing. In other words, it's not what we think or feel that determines our Christlikeness, but what our decisions and actions prove when examined in light of truth. For this reason, we should develop the habit of examining the direction we are traveling and the behaviors we are embracing, from God's perspective.

We can learn to do so from the example in 2 Samuel, chapter 11. Although we don't know the basis for David's decision, the chapter begins by telling us that he remained in the palace when he should have been with his men. Verses 2–3 reveal that during an evening stroll, David saw a woman bathing. We know that his focus lingered long enough to notice that she was very beautiful. He invested further in temptation by sending someone to find out about her (vs. 3): *The man said, "Isn't this Bathsheba, the daughter of Eliam and the wife of Uriah the Hittite?"* In verse 4, David officially sent for the woman and she slept with him. These verses provide evidence that David made deliberate choices to move in a direction that opposed God's will.

Imagine the difference in David's life had he paused to examine or take inventory of his pending personal decisions and actions. Reread these verses, taking note of the multiple opportunities he had to do so. Each of the stages in David's journey demonstrate a change in either direction or action, and could have served as checkpoints for spiritual examination. Since these opportunities were overlooked by David, his behavior pattern continued to oppose God's best for him. As a result of personal choices, David had to eventually repent from a very reactive position (2 Samuel 11:5 through 12:13).

We have the opportunity to learn from David's example. Apart from examining actions and directions from God's perspective, a person will continue to be guided by the flesh. Make no mistake, at any time in his journey David could have made different personal choices. This means that at any time he could have realigned his motives to reflect God's will, moving from a reactive to a proactive position.

In making disciples of others, encourage them that obedience to Christ is developed both through direction and action. In other words, obedience is reflected in whether we are following God's ways and mirroring His character. Teaching them to consistently ask themselves these two significant questions will train them to consider personal obedience: Where am I going? What am I doing? In other words, am I going in the direction God is leading? Are my actions pleasing to Him?

Jeremiah 42:3 records that God's people asked the following of the prophet Jeremiah: *"Pray that the LORD your God will tell us where we should go and what we should do."* We, too, are to rely on God's input throughout the moments of our day to determine whether our direction and actions are pleasing to Him.

Avoid Excuses

In order to consistently correct sinful behavior and prevent future disobedience, we need to purify ourselves from sin rather than excuse it (1 John 3:3). When we try to justify or excuse sinful behavior, we are making obedience contingent on circumstances and conditions rather than on the abiding power of Christ within us. For example, "So I took a few supplies from work; they'll never miss them." "I raised my voice in anger because she provoked me." Even though Jesus is continually gracious to forgive us of undesired behavior, He never lowers His expectations for His followers.

Second Peter 1:3–4 tells us, *His divine power has given us everything we need for life and godliness through our knowledge of him who called us by his own glory and goodness. Through these he has given us his very great and precious promises, so that through them you may participate in the divine nature and escape the corruption in the world caused by evil desires.* Whereas Christ is eternal, the things of this world are only temporal and, therefore, lead to corruption and decay. Verse 4 tells us that the corruption in the world is caused by evil desires. However, many people aren't in the habit of evaluating their desires, let alone willing to classify them as "evil". Evil includes those things that oppose Christ. If we use synonyms for evil such as *sinful* and *selfish*, we can more easily identify ourselves with the source of corruption.

In trying to excuse or justify selfish, sinful behavior, we allow it to continue by ignoring its corrupting effects. This brings us to an important question: If our desires by nature are evil or sinful, why would our holy God allow His Spirit to indwell sinful man? Although desire can be stimulated by something external, the root of desire is internal. By equipping each believer with the indwelling Holy Spirit, He can control our desires at their place of origin—from within. Since God's Spirit is continually available to us and unlimited in every way, we have immediate access to the power to withstand the world's temptations, eliminating a need for excuses.

Titus 2:11–12 says, *For the grace of God that brings salvation has appeared to all men. It teaches us to say "No" to ungodliness and worldly passions, and to live self-controlled, upright and godly lives in this present age.* God's grace enables us to experience spiritual victory here and now. Therefore, rather than trying to justify or excuse behavior that opposes Christ, we can rely on His power to teach us to live self-controlled, upright, and godly lives. Are there any patterns of wrong thinking or wrong behavior that you are currently excusing rather than correcting? If you are a parent, are there individual behaviors in your children that you are attempting to justify or excuse?

In discipling others, teach them that it is often easier to excuse or overlook sinful behavior than it is to correct it. Encourage others to ask the Lord to reveal to them any area of their lives that needs correction rather than human justification. In doing so, they will be allowing God to do a thorough work of both correcting and preventing undesired behavior.

Identify Temptation

It is not temptation itself, but rather acting on or investing in temptation that results in sin. Therefore, it's inaccurate to fully place the blame of personal sin on temptation. Instead, we should identify and learn from past temptations that enticed us to sin in order to guard against future disobedience.

To better understand temptation, we need to realize that temptation does not have its source in God since it does not reflect His nature. James 1:13 tells us, *When tempted, no one should say, "God is tempting me." For God cannot be tempted by evil, nor does he tempt anyone.* Because the source of temptation is evil, the flesh is enticed. This means that even though it's harmful to our spiritual development, temptation may initially appear attractive or pleasurable to our senses.

James 1:14–15 provides us with a word picture of the effects of temptation: *But each one is tempted when, by his own evil desire, he is dragged away and enticed. Then, after desire has conceived, it gives birth to sin; and sin, when it is full-grown, gives birth to death.* Notice that temptation leading to sin is a process and can often become a slippery slope in the life of a believer. For this reason, it's supremely important to learn to identify personal sources of temptation and flee from them. This means that, rather than merely striving to correct sinful behavior, we should ask the Holy Spirit to help us identify the source of temptation that enticed us to sin. Once we've identified the source, we can begin to guard against its alluring effects by removing ourselves from the temptation's influence and by relying on the Lord to enable us to stand firm against it.

Keep in mind that it is often easier to identify sources of temptation in the lives of others than to recognize them in our own lives. Inviting the Holy Spirit to point out areas of temptation in your life may reveal things you may have otherwise never considered or, perhaps, falsely believed to be within acceptable limits. First Corinthians 10:12 warns us, *So, if you think you are standing firm, be careful that you don't fall!* Rather than assume that we are standing firmly against temptation, we are to be continually humble and open to the Spirit's revelation concerning sources of potential temptation.

First Corinthians 10:13 says, *No temptation has seized you except what is common to man. And God is faithful; he will not let you be tempted beyond what you can bear. But when you are tempted, he will also provide a way out so that you can stand up under it.* There is no temptation that is uncommon to mankind and, even in the most challenging temptations, God will never allow us to be tempted beyond what we can withstand in His strength.

The Lord will faithfully enable us to be triumphant over temptation and sin by providing us with a way to withstand it or a means of escape. Too often people fall into sin because they fail to recognize or pursue a means of escape during the temptation. For this reason, in addition to identifying specific sources of temptation, we are to rely on the discernment and strength of the Holy Spirit to reveal a means of escape and then pursue it.

In discipling others, let them know that Christ not only desires to correct sinful behavior but also will empower us to overcome future temptation and sin as we depend on Him to do so. Proverbs 4:26–27 instructs us, *Make level paths for your feet and take only ways that are firm. Do not swerve to the right or the left; keep your foot from evil.* Even though we may be confronted with temptation, through knowledge of truth and reliance on the power of God, we can avoid investing in it.

Since God has purpose in all things, we should avoid leaving any part of our lives to chance. God has laid out a plan for successful living through His Word and has equipped us with the power of the Holy Spirit to enable us to walk in the victory obedience provides. Explain to others that pursuing Christ involves actively searching His Word and taking personal initiative to apply truth in specific areas of our lives, resulting in victory over temptation and sin.

CHAPTER TWENTY-ONE

Applying Truth in Choices and Consequences

Throughout each day, we are continually presented with choices. Although some decisions may seem insignificant, many choices we face have the potential for eternal significance and some can result in lifelong consequences. For these reasons, it's crucial that we learn to recognize and carefully consider choices and their potential consequences from God's perspective.

While some people find it unreasonable to include God in every moment of the day, there is a question that needs to be asked and answered. In what areas of our lives does God not want to be involved? Psalm 139:1–4 says, *O LORD, you have searched me and you know me. You know when I sit and when I rise; you perceive my thoughts from afar. You discern my going out and my lying down; you are familiar with all my ways. Before a word is on my tongue you know it completely,*

O LORD. God is all-knowing and intimately aware of the details of our lives. Even so, it is through the invitation to include Him in our decision-making process that He becomes personally involved in the details of our lives. Is it your habit to involve God in your decision-making process?

The Bible teaches that each person will reap what they sow (Galatians 6:7). This means that, even though the consequences may be eventual rather than immediate, we will each experience consequences resulting from personal choices. Galatians 6:8 tells us, *The one who sows to please his sinful nature, from that nature will reap destruction; the one who sows to please the Spirit, from the Spirit will reap eternal life.* The farmer who chooses to plant corn shouldn't expect to harvest beans, since the consequence, or end result, of planting corn is a harvest of corn.

As you can see, reaping and sowing are both based on choices. Sowing is the action that results from a personal choice, and reaping is the consequence that results from choosing to act. Each choice provides opportunity to sow those things that gratify the flesh, or to invest in the things that please the Spirit. If you haven't been trained to consider choices, you also may not think about potential consequences resulting from possible choices. Regardless, what we decide to do with each choice can indeed determine whether the outcome is honoring to God. The following methods of application will help you learn practical ways of examining choices and potential consequences from God's perspective.

Recognize and Acknowledge Choices

If we want to include God in our decision-making process, we must first train ourselves to consistently recognize choices. In doing so, we can then seek God's perspective. Look at Jeremiah 6:16: *This is what the LORD says, "Stand at the crossroads. . ."* The crossroads represent a point of decision, an opportunity for personal choice concerning a future course of direction.

The Lord wants us to learn to stand, or pause, prior to making a decision in order to accurately consider His viewpoint. Since it's possible for us to be physically still while our minds and emotions are racing, choosing to stand refers to intentionally placing our thoughts and emotions in a holding pattern. In other words, to place yourself in a pause position is to be in a state of neutral, causing thoughts and emotions to be without movement in any direction. Think about it. If we fail to pause for considering God's perspective, we may invest in thoughts and feelings that move us in one direction over another. By automatically following personal thoughts and feelings, we are led by the flesh rather than by the Spirit. Pausing to involve God in our choices throughout the day is choosing to be proactive in our pursuit of pleasing Him.

If it isn't already your habit, begin including the Lord in your decision-making process by asking Him to enable you to recognize personal choices throughout your day. Then, begin pausing to consider His perspective. You may initially find that you begin to recognize choices after you've made them. In addition, you may find that even though you're beginning to recognize choices, you fail to consider God's perspective prior to making the choice. Because this spiritual discipline requires practice, focus on its benefits rather than becoming frustrated with the initial process. As you consistently give God control over your decisions, you'll begin to identify more and more opportunities to involve Him in the process.

In discipling others, encourage them to ask the Lord to help them recognize and seize opportunities to invite Him to be a part of their decision-making process. Then, ask each person you disciple to think about all they have learned to this point. Discuss what the discipline of pausing to allow God's input in their life might accomplish:

- The position of neutral acknowledges God's authority in our lives and represents our desire to surrender to His will.
- A neutral position allows the Holy Spirit to evaluate our motives and intentions so that we can align them with His, prior to action.
- Being in neutral also allows us to consider the potential eternal purpose in each choice.
- It provides opportunity to consider the truth of God's Word and His nature. In doing so, we can then act confidently on absolute truth rather than follow selfish thoughts or waver in indecision.

Encourage others to focus on the benefits of putting themselves in a position of neutral to consider God's perspective as they make decisions.

Seek with Intention

Now that we've learned the benefits of recognizing choices and pausing at points of decision, let's return to Jeremiah 6:16: *This is what the LORD says, "Stand at the crossroads and look;. . ."* Consider this: When a person in authority tells a pilot to postpone their landing, the pilot puts the airplane in a holding pattern. Even though the pilot suspends a flight in midair, they are still actively flying the plane as they await further instruction. Similarly, God asks us to place ourselves in a position of neutral while at the same time being intentionally active in our pursuit of Him. In other words, God wants us to be purposeful as we remain in neutral until we receive direction from Him to move forward.

Rather than consider moving in our own direction, God asks us to stop and look intentionally for the direction in which He is leading. As Christ-followers, we want to follow closely in His steps rather than get ahead of what the Lord is doing or lag so far behind that we can't see Him. To do so, we'll need to consistently be looking in His direction as we await His Spirit's next instruction.

In discipling others, explain that Christ-followers are to be intentional in setting their gaze on the Lord. Keeping their focus on Jesus, rather than on self, will enable believers to recognize His will.

Ask with Purpose

As we actively await God's leading, we are to be intentionally looking and asking for His guidance. Read again Jeremiah 6:16: *This is what the LORD says, "Stand at the crossroads and look; ask for the ancient paths, ask where the good way is,. . ."*

Even though the written Word was not readily available to God's people in the Old Testament, the Israelites passed down the truth of His eternal qualities and instructions from generation to generation. Jeremiah instructed them to "ask for the ancient paths," to bring to remembrance what happened to God's people when they chose to be obedient and when they followed their own desires. Since God never changes, by looking back, they could learn to identify and walk in His faithfulness. Jeremiah also encouraged them to "ask where the good way is," the obedient or perfect way of God. Although God has a perfect plan for our lives, He won't force us to follow His directives. He will often wait for us to willingly include Him in our lives.

We can practice remaining in a neutral position while looking and asking for God's guidance, using spiritually discerning questions. For example: Does the Bible have anything to say about the subject being considered? How does this decision represent God's best? Does this choice reflect the character of God? In what ways will this decision bring honor to the Lord and please Him? Questions such as these can promote thought from God's perspective, concerning both potential choices and consequences.

In discipling others, teach them that to learn God's will we must be in the habit of inquiring of Him. To "stand, look, and ask" is to stop and consider who God is and what obedience to Him looks like. This same discipline can be achieved today to consider God's best for our lives.

Walk in Obedience

Remember, without application there is no change. This means that we may learn to recognize choices, place ourselves in neutral, and ask for God's guidance; and yet still fail to follow His will. With the need for application in mind, let's return to Jeremiah 6:16: *This is what the LORD says: "Stand at the crossroads and look; ask for the ancient paths, ask where the good way is, and walk in it,. . ."* Apart from the choice to implement God's truth in our daily lives, transformation will not result. Therefore, diligently pursue truth with the purpose of personal application.

In discipling others, remind them that it is not enough to merely consider God's will. We must be willing to allow Him to effectively implement it in our lives. By doing so, we walk in a manner that pleases and honors Him.

Rest in the Lord

Let's return once again to Jeremiah 6:16: *This is what the LORD says: "Stand at the crossroads and look; ask for the ancient paths, ask where the good way is, and walk in it, and you will find rest for your souls."* What a joy it is to know that God promises to bless those who follow His ways!

In discipling others, remind them that God always keeps His promises. While the world around us is often confused and chaotic, He promises to provide abiding peace and rest for the journey to those who walk with Him.

Test for the Best

It is always God's desire to reveal His absolute best for His children rather than have them settle for what is merely good or better (Isaiah 48:17; Philippians 1:9–11). In order to consistently recognize God's best for us, we need to develop a lifestyle that tests, or examines, personal choices in light of His truth rather than depend on our guesses or assumptions.

Romans 12:2 says, *Do not conform any longer to the pattern of this world, but be transformed by the renewing of your mind. Then you will be able to test and approve what God's will is—his good, pleasing and perfect will.* Notice the order God gives us for knowing His will. We must first choose to no longer allow the world's pattern of thinking to affect us, but instead transform our way of thinking by consistently renewing our minds with truth. This is of extreme importance and takes daily, diligent practice.

The world's point of view is subjective and ever changing. God's point of view is objective, absolute, and never changing. Therefore, using God's Word as our standard produces objectivity. In the same way construction workers set a plumb line as an objective standard to ensure that a building is built square and true, God provides a plumb line for His people to ensure their lives are structurally sound and in line with His will (Amos 7:7–8). Using truth as a standard to test circumstances will reveal God's best choices.

So what kind of situations should be tested? First Thessalonians 5:21–22 tells us, *Test everything. Hold on to the good. Avoid every kind of evil.* Since God means what He says and says what He means, we are to develop a lifestyle of testing all things. By using truth as the testing standard, God will reveal to us those things that represent Him and those things that do not. We can then confidently take hold of those things that please God, while avoiding the rest. Although this spiritual discipline will require practice, the resulting benefits will be well worth the effort.

In addition to testing life situations, we are to practice examining information by comparing it to biblical truth (1 John 4:1). Remember, information can be encountered without ever being received. We are to rely on the Holy Spirit to help us discern between those things that mirror God's Word and His character and those things that do not. Then we are to follow only those things that reflect Christ.

Since our words can and should affect others, it's essential that our input reflects biblical truth. For this reason, it is helpful to practice evaluating the content of your conversations for truth. If you are linking your words to biblical principles, then your conversation is reflecting God's Word and His nature. If, however, your words fail to connect to biblical truth, then it's likely they represent personal opinion. Ask God to make you sensitive to the words you use and enable you to lovingly and effectively speak truth.

In discipling others, it's beneficial to link the instruction you provide to biblical principles. This will help others learn to do so for themselves. For example, let's presume that you're mentoring a parent who is experiencing difficulty in getting their teen to clean their room. Because this request often results in strife between parent and child, the parent wants to know if the request is unreasonable.

Respond by asking the parent to test their instructions using truth to consider whether or not their request can be linked to biblical principles. For instance, the Bible tells us that God is a god of order and desires each area of our lives to be orderly rather than chaotic, including our living spaces. Also, God wants us to be good stewards of all He's given us. In allowing our rooms to become messy, we waste time trying to find things and take a chance of losing or breaking valuables. Encourage the parent to instruct their son using biblical principles, rather than personal opinion, knowing that in doing so they will be training their son in godliness.

Because a lifestyle that tests everything will take effort, talk to the person you are mentoring about the blessings that will result. Encourage them that dividing good from evil and pure from impure presents a choice of obedience. Help them to see that, as they choose to live proactively by testing situations using truth, they will reap the benefits of obedience.

Certainty in the Uncertain

Yet another way to help us identify God's best in our daily decisions is to develop the habit of dividing out those things that we know to be true from those that are uncertain. This method of applying truth is evident in the life of Abraham, as seen in Genesis 22:1: *Some time later God tested Abraham. He said to him, "Abraham!" "Here I am," he replied.* Abraham recognized God's voice as a result of his intimate relationship with Him. Also, Abraham's immediate response to God reflects a heart surrendered, ready to receive God's instruction and obey His will. These elements of abiding and surrender are significant in recognizing God's will in the decision-making process.

Now read Genesis 22:2: Then God said, *"Take your son, your only son, Isaac, whom you love, and go to the region of Moriah. Sacrifice him there as a burnt offering on one of the mountains I will tell you about."* Notice that God provided Abraham with detailed instructions concerning his son and general instructions concerning the direction he was to go. God also intentionally withheld some instructions to be revealed at a future, undisclosed time. Verses 3–4 reveal that Abraham did exactly as God had told him. As with Abraham, when God provides us with instruction, we are obedient by acting only on what He shows us, nothing more and nothing less.

Now look at Genesis 22:6–8: *Abraham took the wood for the burnt offering and placed it on his son Isaac, and he himself carried the fire and the knife. As the two of them went on together, Isaac spoke up and said to his father Abraham, "Father?"*

"Yes, my son?" Abraham replied.

"The fire and wood are here," Isaac said, "but where is the lamb for the burnt offering?"

Abraham answered, "God himself will provide the lamb for the burnt offering, my son." And the two of them went on together." There is much to be learned from this passage of Scripture.

First of all, Abraham only acted on what he knew to be true from God's instructions and His character. When we receive instruction from the Lord, we, too, can proceed by faith trusting that His ways are best. Secondly, Abraham didn't hesitate to let Isaac know that he didn't have all the answers but was trusting God's character to provide and guide. We can also be prepared to respond to others with confidence in God's promises rather than appear doubtful because we don't have all the answers.

Comments such as these reflect faith in the midst of unknowns: "I'm not sure what I'll be doing next, but I know God will reveal His will to me in His perfect timing, and I'm content to wait on Him." "I don't have all the answers but I know God does, and I'm trusting Him to lead the way." By dividing out the truth you are certain of from those things that are uncertain, it becomes easier to recognize and embrace truth with confidence. Then, rather than wondering or worrying about the unknown, you can choose to release it to God's care.

Finally, although God withheld information from him, Abraham continued on the path of obedience with confidence in God. Similarly, as we walk confidently by the leading of the Holy Spirit, we can rest not only in what He is currently showing us but also in what will be revealed to us as we trust.

In discipling others, teach them to recognize choices to walk in obedience by dividing out revealed truth from speculative thought. Encourage them to walk confidently in the truth God reveals and to patiently await His continued guidance. To foster a deeper reliance on Him, God will always allow unknowns in our lives. In those times, when a person is living in obedience to Christ but not receiving instruction from Him, encourage them to faithfully follow the last instruction given as they await God's timing and leading (Psalm 27:14; Isaiah 64:4).

But God

As we've learned in previous chapters, using transitional phrases can be helpful in bridging the gap between recognizing truth and the choice to walk in it. Learning to use the phrase, "But God" will assist us in transitioning from considering truth in our personal choices to applying it. For example, we know that our thoughts, feelings, and emotions, although very real, don't always reflect truth. In order to walk securely in truth, we must avoid what may appear to be true to embrace what is actually true. Consider Jacob and his brother, Esau, in the Old Testament. After deceiving Esau, Jacob fled from him for many years. Genesis 32:7 records Jacob preparing to reunite with his brother. Although Jacob had a relationship with the Lord, he experienced fear and distress because he was uncertain of how Esau would respond to his return.

In Genesis 32:11–12, Jacob prayed to God concerning his predicament: *"Save me, I pray, from the hand of my brother Esau, for I am afraid he will come and attack me, and also the mothers with their children. But you have said, 'I will surely make you prosper and will make your descendants like the sand of the sea, which cannot be counted.'"* In the midst of his great fear, Jacob made two significant decisions: he turned to the One powerful enough to banish all fear, and he reminded himself of truth. The choice to do so is noted in the use of the transitional phrase "but you [God]."

In another example, Psalm 73:26 says, *My flesh and my heart may fail, but God is the strength of my heart and my portion forever.* Human beings fail. But, rather than become discouraged or defeated, the Psalmist transitions from what he is thinking to absolute truth by using the phrase, "But God." In doing so, he reaffirms his confidence in God, choosing to rest securely in Him. You, too, can practice using the phrase "but God" to aid in recognizing and walking in truth.

In discipling others, be aware that people can be comfortable sharing honestly about their thoughts and feelings, but may fail to transition to applying truth in their situation. Encourage them to renew their minds with truth by using the phrase, "But God." Lovingly remind them that any delay in choosing to stand on God's promises creates greater risk for distraction and the potential to walk in the flesh rather than in truth.

At this point, the person you are mentoring is most likely striving to diligently apply many biblical principles in their life. Continue to encourage them to commit each work to the Lord, allowing Him to create and achieve permanent change within their heart and life. Remind them that the benefits of being able to recognize God's will in their daily choices far outweigh the cost of training.

CHAPTER TWENTY-TWO

Applying Truth in Relationships

God designed each of us to have relationships with people, and He has enormous purpose in how He wants us to interact and bond with others. Relationships create an avenue in which people can influence our lives, and we can influence the lives of others. Are you in the habit of considering the influence individual relationships have in your life? What about the lives of your children?

People use a variety of words to describe relationships such as *casual*, *professional*, *romantic*, *intimate*, *family*, *broken*, *unhealthy*, and even *abusive*. It can be challenging to evaluate each relationship objectively because human emotions and personal perspectives can get in the way. Yet, apart from evaluating or testing each relationship, how will we know whether or not they are pleasing to the Lord? For this reason, it's crucial that we learn to evaluate personal relationships and do so using God's objective viewpoint—truth. As we apply God's truth in relationships, we'll grow to see people from His perspective, develop godly friendships, and consistently react to others in a Christlike manner.

To help us understand God's will concerning relationships, it is beneficial to recognize and consider the two types of relationships we experience: chosen and unchosen. Chosen relationships are those unions we willingly enter into; unchosen relationships are those created apart from our choosing. However, it's significant to realize that even in unchosen relationships, we have a choice in how we act and respond to others.

Chosen Relationships

Consider how friendships, dating relationships, marriages, business partners, and roommates are possible examples of chosen relationships or unions. Understanding God's perspective on chosen unions will equip us to make godly choices concerning them. For example, 2 Corinthians 6:14–15 tells us, *Do not be yoked together with unbelievers. For what do righteousness and wickedness have in common? Or what fellowship can light have with darkness? What harmony is there between Christ and Belial? What does a believer have in common with an unbeliever?*

When a relationship is established, a connection or initial bond is made. Over a period of time, a strong bond, even if initially unintentional, can develop. Make no mistake: The greater the connection or bond developed within each relationship, the greater the influence. For this reason, Paul instructs us to abstain from allowing ourselves to be yoked, or bonded together, with unbelievers.

A yoke is a wooden frame used to join two animals together in order to increase effectiveness. In Deuteronomy 22:10, God commanded His people not to plow with an ox and a donkey yoked together. The difference in their size and strides could make one animal uncomfortable while possibly choking the other or causing it to be dragged behind. As you can imagine, this would be unprofitable for the animals and their work. Conversely, when two animals of the same species are yoked together, their union doesn't cause conflict and they are able to accomplish great work.

God uses this practical illustration to teach us about relationships. The yoke represents the union of two people, or a relationship. Two people both pursuing personal righteousness are united in Christ. Therefore, their relationship can be considered equally yoked. As a result, God enables each to complement and enhance the efforts of the other. In contrast, a union between a believer and an unbeliever is, according to Scripture, unequally yoked because their spiritual pursuits are dissimilar.

We can test the equality of a yoke using truth-provoking questions: Is the person you are befriending pursuing righteousness? Are they consistently seeking God's will for their life? Are they striving to follow Christ through their patterns of behavior? Since relationships have enormous potential to influence the way we think and act, we should carefully consider each personal bond. It's a person's actions, rather than their words, that reflect what they genuinely believe (Proverbs 20:11). Therefore, we should practice evaluating a person's lifestyle rather than considering only their words. This means that our basis for close relationships is to be current, rather than potential behavior.

Our loving God designed relationships between people to be both meaningful and purposeful. Ecclesiastes 4:9–10 says, *Two are better than one, because they have a good return for their work: If one falls down, his friend can help him up. But pity the man who falls and has no one to help him up!* This verse reminds us of the value of genuine friendships and the purpose in companionship.

God never intended for us to be isolated; He wants us to have friends. But remember, God is a god of order. Therefore, it's wise to enter into and develop relationships in a spiritually beneficial order. This means that a potentially godly relationship will begin with getting acquainted, before developing a friendship or an even deeper relationship—while you are carefully guarding your heart. In doing so, you will prevent emotions and feelings from getting in the way of what God wants to reveal to you, concerning each association.

Although society leads us to believe that we should follow our hearts, Scripture instructs us to make it a priority to guard our hearts. Proverbs 4:23 tells us, *Above all else, guard your heart, for it is the wellspring of life.* God wants us to recognize our hearts as the wellspring of life. This means that our hearts hold everything of value and importance to our very being and, therefore, should be carefully guarded.

Because it's difficult to reverse the consequences of an unguarded heart, God wants each of us to develop the qualities of a well-guarded heart:

- One who guards their heart is on duty and alert to potential danger.
- A person with a guarded heart examines potential relationships from God's perspective.
- Those with guarded hearts use God's truth to filter any potential impurities, refusing to entertain impure thoughts or impure motives.
- One who carefully watches their heart is not easily persuaded by the world, or enticed to go anywhere the Lord does not lead.
- One who purposefully protects their heart will consistently choose

to exchange fleshly desires for those that please Christ.

- A person with a safeguarded heart will not base decisions on feelings, but instead on careful consideration of God's Word and perfect will.

Since a person who has guarded their heart does not choose to enter into relationships based on emotions, they don't risk the chance of their heart becoming broken. Those who truly desire to please the Lord will keep their hearts safely guarded while establishing and developing relationships.

So, what do Christ-centered relationships look like? In Philippians 2:1–2 Paul wrote, *If you have any encouragement from being united with Christ, if any comfort from his love, if any fellowship with the Spirit, if any tenderness and compassion, then make my joy complete by being like-minded, having the same love, being one in spirit and purpose.* Notice that Paul's instructions are for God's people to be like-minded, united in spirit and purpose. This means that it's not enough to merely enjoy similar interests or activities, but moreover the common bond in any relationship should be the love of Christ. As a result, believers should be united in pursuing God's Spirit and purpose for their lives. This mutual agreement concerning the things of God is the like-mindedness Paul is referring to and reflects God's will in establishing friendships as well as deeper relationships.

As you can see, considering relationships based on truth enables us to be proactive in developing godly friendships. For example, Proverbs 17:17 tells us, *A friend loves at all times, and a brother is born for adversity.* We can identify a godly friend as one who conveys unconditional love as Jesus does. A godly friend will also be trustworthy and loyal in good times and bad. Hebrews 10:24 says, *And let us consider how we may spur one another on toward love and good deeds.* Here we learn that a Christ-centered friend puts others first rather than demanding their own way. They consider ways to encourage others in the Lord and help further develop their character and service to Christ.

Proverbs 27:17 says, *As iron sharpens iron, so one man sharpens another.* A godly friend will not hesitate to communicate truth to their friends, even though it may be difficult to say and to receive. They will strive, in love, to hold friends accountable to live according to the character of Christ. Is it your heart's desire to have godly friendships? Where are you going and what are you doing to establish and develop Christ-centered friendships? In what ways are you developing the personal traits of a godly companion?

If it isn't already your habit, practice distinguishing the traits of ungodly and godly influences. As light in this dark world, we will consistently be surrounded by the lost. However, we cannot afford to allow ungodliness to influence our walk with Jesus. To put it simply: An ungodly influence is one who tempts you to think, speak, or act contrary to Scripture. Allowing ungodly influences to impact our lives is never God's best. We pursue God's very best by choosing relationships that please Him and represent truth. We are to also develop relationships that help hold us accountable to live according to truth. Begin asking God to develop within you the qualities of a godly companion, to provide you with godly relationships, and to enable you to recognize them.

In discipling others, show them the enormous worth of Christ-centered relationships. Since building and maintaining such relationships can be challenging for some people, it may be beneficial to train others to identify and appreciate the differences between an acquaintance and a genuine friend. An acquaintance may be someone with whom a person attends school, works, or periodically socializes—who does not have a large influence in their life. A friend, however, is someone with whom they have built a relationship, one who does have influence, or directly impacts their life. This also includes any relationship that becomes deeper than a friendship. Teach others to recognize godly relationships as those that have God's best interest in mind and to consistently reevaluate relationships that do not.

Also teach others to distinguish between influencing and being influenced by others. First Corinthians 15:33 says, *Do not be misled: "Bad company corrupts good character."* Encourage them to avoid unequally yoked relationships and to enter into unions that promote growth in their walk with Jesus. If the principle of godly relationships is new to the person you are mentoring, they may need assistance in recognizing ungodly relationships in their life. In the case of a suspected ungodly alliance, point them to the evidence and discuss the potential consequences of such a relationship. With these thoughts in mind, remember that teaching others to be proactive, rather than reactive, in chosen relationships reflects God's best.

There may be times when the person you're mentoring desires a dating or marriage relationship. Rather than pursue a love relationship and get ahead of God's will, advise them to commit this issue to prayer and to wait patiently on God to work on their behalf. Further encourage them to continually pursue godly wisdom by studying what the Bible has to say about godly women and wives, and godly men and husbands. Show them how to use their concordance to help with this study and encourage them to make a list of the attributes that apply. In doing so, each person will be proactive in developing personal godly attributes and becoming equipped to recognize godly attributes in others.

Unchosen Relationships

In addition to those relationships we choose to enter into, some relationships are not chosen unions. This means that there will be times when God specifically places us among believers as well as unbelievers regardless of personal choice. There may be times in your life, for example, when you don't have a direct choice concerning relationships such as family members, co-workers, or classmates. In these situations, as in all situations, Christ-followers are obligated to walk in obedience. Therefore, if we find ourselves struggling with a relationship we didn't choose to enter into, we should seek purpose in it by considering God's perspective and applying truth. As a result, we can truly live victoriously through challenging relationships.

A relationship most often becomes challenging as a result of conflict, resulting from any number of things: a difference of opinion, miscommunication, distrust, anger, or pride. The enemy uses conflict to create disunity and strife, but Jesus desires unity and peace. Consequently, we should deal successfully with conflict by first learning to recognize the source of each struggle. Ephesians 6:12 says, *For our struggle is not against flesh and blood, but against the rulers, against the authorities, against the powers of this dark world and against the spiritual forces of evil in the heavenly realms.*

The truth is, that our struggles are not with other human beings. This verse reveals that every struggle is spiritual. Therefore, the source of all conflict is biblical truth versus self-will. (It's extremely valuable to realize that, regardless of the apparent issue, there is only one source!) Since a focus on truth results in unity, when a conflict results, at least one person is pursuing their own way. This means that if you are pursuing truth, rather than self, there is no need to take personally the issue. Instead, you should practice focusing on truth rather than on the person engaged in the struggle. This will enable you to keep an objective perspective and prevent you from being distracted or offended.

In dealing with a fellow believer, we should try to lovingly resolve an issue by using the truth of God's character and His Word. In contrast, an unbeliever may not recognize truth. Even so, we are to convey truth in love by the leading of the Holy Spirit (1 Corinthians 13:1; Galatians 5:25).

At times, a relationship can be difficult because people can dislike other people. Sadly, some people choose to be enemies regardless of our actions. As a result, there will be those who will not respond to any amount of love and kindness shown to them. In these cases, we should remember that God's love is unconditional; it doesn't depend on our actions or response to Him. Therefore, in honor of Jesus, our love for others shouldn't depend on their actions toward us. In Luke 6:27–28 Jesus said, *"But I tell you who hear me: Love your enemies, do good to those who hate you, bless those who curse you, pray for those who mistreat you."*

Even though Jesus was perfect and loving in every way, He was mistreated by His enemies. He was unjustly insulted, mocked, spat upon, beaten, and hated by those who opposed Him. What did Jesus do? He loved them anyway. People who choose to hate, rather than love, don't understand Jesus or the depth of His love for them. This realization should motivate us to show greater compassion to those who oppose us. Although enemies can be difficult to love, we should fully rely on the power of the Holy Spirit to enable us to convey Christ's love to even our worst enemies. In addition, Jesus instructed us to pray for our enemies (Matthew 5:43–48). If it isn't already your habit, begin earnestly praying for your enemies, asking God to draw each of them closer to Jesus.

At times relationships can be challenging because others may not respect or agree with our biblical beliefs and convictions. We can be encouraged by 1 John 3:1: *How great is the love the Father has lavished on us, that we should be called children of God!* And that is what we are! The reason the world does not know us is that it did not know him.

It makes sense that those who don't have a personal relationship with Jesus may have difficulty relating to those who do. For this reason, we should pray for those who oppose our faith, asking God to do a mighty work in their lives. In doing so, we will please the Lord and increase in love for them.

There may be times when a person struggles in a relationship with a governing authority in their life. Romans 13:1 says, *Everyone must submit himself to the governing authorities, for there is no authority except that which God has established. The authorities that exist have been established by God.* Although this verse is referring to civil authorities, the principle can also apply to other authorities. For example, employers manage their employees, teachers oversee students, etc. The Bible teaches that governing authorities that exist have been established by God, not man.

Although it may appear that man appoints those in positions of authority, it is actually God who has ultimate control. For instance, you may vote for officials to occupy government positions. However, because God is sovereign, He has ultimate control in determining positions of leadership; and those in authority will be accountable to Him.

Even though the Bible instructs us to submit to authorities, the Lord rules over all. Therefore, His Word is to be the ultimate authority in our lives. Acts 5:29 records the apostles' reply to the authorities of their time: *"We must obey God rather than men!"* God wants us to obediently submit to those in authority over us, unless their instructions fail to line up with His truth. Since God is the highest authority, we can't agree to submit to anyone who asks us to compromise truth. If you find yourself in this situation, ask His Spirit to provide you with specific wisdom and direction to know what to do.

In even the most challenging relationships, Jesus wants His followers to represent Him. For example, Jesus is the Prince of Peace. Therefore, we should strive, as much as possible, to live at peace with everyone. Romans 12:18 says, *If it is possible, as far as it depends on you, live at peace with everyone.* Although we cannot make other people live at peace with us, we have a choice whether or not to live peaceably with others. This means that a person may choose to ridicule us, but we don't have to choose to receive personal ridicule or engage in defending ourselves. Instead, we should practice various ways to avoid an argument. Rather than argue, become angry, or fight, we can rely on the power of the Holy Spirit to enable us to remain calm, under His control, and at peace with others.

As we depend more fully on the power of God's Spirit, He will guide us in the appropriate response—whether to be quiet, walk away from the situation, or speak. In Matthew 5:9 Jesus said, *"Blessed are the peacemakers, for they will be called sons of God."* The life of Jesus is the best example of peace displayed in conflict. Living at peace with others is choosing to live as Jesus did.

In discipling others, help them to see that God has purpose in unchosen relationships, even challenging ones. If the person you are mentoring is finding a relationship difficult, show them ways that God may use the situation to develop deeper personal dependence on Jesus. Encourage them to persist in prayer and the study of God's Word when seeking specific direction in dealing with conflict. Also, advise them to be prepared to speak truth in love as God provides opportunity.

There may be times when you mentor someone who is having difficulty with a relationship due to past or current rejection. Although it's very difficult for someone to be rejected by those who should love them most, God will sustain them. In this case, encourage the person by reading Psalm 27:10: *Though my father and mother forsake me, the*

LORD will receive me. Remind them that everything they can possibly need is found in our loving, compassionate God. Let them know that moving past hurt and toward victory begins as we allow Jesus to transform us through His comfort, forgiveness of others, and healing.

Although it will not be easy, encourage them to turn each offense over to the Lord rather than continuing to focus on the hurt created by others. In doing so, they will be choosing to live victoriously in Jesus by allowing Him to deal fully with each disappointment. Further encourage them to cease depending on others for any kind of fulfillment and to turn to God at all times, trusting Him for all things. Teach them to ask God to prepare them in advance of their next encounter, so they will know what to say and do.

Whether or not a relationship is chosen, God desires to be honored through it. For this reason, we are to view relationships from Christ's perspective, practice His principles, and leave the results with Him.

CHAPTER TWENTY-THREE

Applying Truth in Adversity

If you've ever experienced personal adversity, then you know that talking or studying about adversity is not the same as living through it. If you have not yet experienced adversity, understand that none of us are immune to the trials of life, and they can strike without warning. Yet through each hardship, our precious Lord Jesus is with us to comfort, guide, and provide victory.

Just to clarify, some hardships in life are the consequences of poor choices, whereas others are not. It is significant to learn to distinguish the two and respond accordingly. Let's first consider that there may be times when we suffer as a direct or indirect result of personal choices. Even though God forgives us when we make decisions outside His will, sometimes the adverse consequences of sin remain.

If we fail to consider whether or not we are experiencing difficulties as a natural consequence of personal decisions, we may also fail to take responsibility and learn from them. In addition, we could potentially repeat behavior and incur similar suffering. In these instances, we should seek God's forgiveness and rely on Him to help us correct future behavior. Is it your habit to ask the Lord to reveal any personal responsibility you may have for actions that led to adverse circumstances?

Also, the Bible teaches that we will each undergo difficulties that result from life experiences unrelated to the consequences of personal sin. The remainder of this chapter will address these types of adversities. Since God has eternal purpose in personal hardship, He wants us to learn how to apply truth in adverse circumstances.

Adversity comes in various forms and can affect any aspect of our life. For example, a variety of trials can occur on a daily basis. These are short-term and can, if we allow them to, leave us frustrated, fearful, worried, and doubtful. Some people experience chronic adversity—months or even seasons of hardship such as a long-term illness or unemployment. Yet, other adversities are acute in nature; their effects are great and sudden as in a medical emergency, natural disaster, or unexpected death.

Regardless of the type of adversity, the afflictions of life will typically reveal two things about each of us: what we really believe to be true about God and those specific spiritual issues that are unsettled in our lives. To be sure, it's very difficult to settle spiritual issues in the midst of adversity because, in those moments, emotional influence can be very strong. Apart from activating our faith, human nature will avoid pain, anguish, or suffering rather than pursue God's purpose in it. What would others say is your typical reaction when faced with adversity?

Don't misunderstand: Walking by faith in adversity doesn't take away stress or grief. But it does change our perspective. In 2 Corinthians 4:8–9 Paul wrote, *We are hard pressed on every side, but not crushed; perplexed, but not in despair; persecuted, but not abandoned; struck down, but not destroyed.* It isn't the adversity, but rather a response grounded in truth that reveals Christ's power in us.

When faced with adversity, Jesus expects His followers to act differently than the world. For example, the Bible teaches that we are not to grieve as those who have no hope (1 Thessalonians 4:13). It doesn't say that we aren't to grieve, but the way we express grief should reveal our trust in God's promises. In fact, if we desire to be triumphant, especially in seasons of adversity, we will need to learn to stand on the promises of God. For this reason, become familiar with the application of the following promises to become as proactive as possible concerning adversity.

Purpose in Adversity

God demonstrates His love by providing us with His Word and making it applicable for every situation, so we can learn to prevent being caught off guard by circumstances. In John 16:33 Jesus said, *"I have told you these things, so that in me you may have peace. In this world you will have trouble. But take heart! I have overcome the world."* To be certain, each and every one of us will experience potentially stressful and challenging times. As a result of knowing this truth, we shouldn't be surprised by such occasions. This verse reveals an option to experience peace in the midst of adversity by choosing to abide in Christ. Because of Jesus' victory over sin and death, we can confidently secure complete victory over the troubles of this world!

Romans 8:28 says, *And we know that in all things God works for the good of those who love him, who have been called according to his purpose.* It's challenging to fathom how God can work each individual situation in this vast world for good. However, in choosing to trust in God's truth, we can expect Him to accomplish all He says He will do. Because the world has nothing in common with the truth of God's Word, its view of good, bad, just, and unjust is vastly different from that of God's.

If we take the world's view, we may consider some situations to be unfair and doubt that good can result from difficulty; yet doubt and despair fail to reflect a life of faith. God works for the good of those who love Him. This means that even though a situation may appear unjust, God may use it to build character or perseverance. An unexplained hardship, although challenging, isn't viewed negatively when we realize that our loving God is using it to produce a deeper reliance and trust in Him. An unexpected trial, though difficult, becomes purposeful when we recognize that God is working in it to increase our faith.

James 1:2–4 tells us, *Consider it pure joy, my brothers, whenever you face trials of many kinds, because you know that the testing of your faith develops perseverance. Perseverance must finish its work so that you may be mature and complete, not lacking anything.* As humans, it is unnatural to embrace seasons of difficulty. Therefore, if we desire to experience spiritual victory, we must recognize and accept God's enormous purpose in the trials of life:

- Since nothing is too hard for God, adversity trains us to rely fully on His power.
- A true test of faith occurs in trying times.
- Perseverance produces spiritual maturity.
- We can experience true joy, knowing that God is in complete control and is working to fulfill His will in us.

In discipling others, explain that even though He may not create personal hardship, God will allow it for His greater purpose. Through trust in Jesus, we can confidently endure and overcome hardship as He did. Help others to see that the world views trouble as negative, yet God sees it as an opportunity to bring Himself glory. Standing on God's promises and power, while enduring adversity, brings honor and glory to the name of Jesus.

Suffering

Sometimes adversity comes by means of suffering: the physical pain of illness, emotional distress due to a personal crisis, or mental anguish as a result of sudden tragedy. Although this teaching may be challenging to receive, the truth is that the Lord allows us to experience suffering for His greater purposes.

God will allow personal suffering to draw us to seek solace and reassurance in Him. Second Corinthians 1:3–4 says, *Praise be to the God and Father of our Lord Jesus Christ, the Father of compassion and the God of all comfort, who comforts us in all our troubles, so that we can comfort those in any trouble with the comfort we ourselves have received from God.* Imagine, each experience of being consoled by our precious Lord enables us to better convey God's comfort to others. Also, personal adversity gives us understanding and insight useful in helping others endure similar situations. As a result, each experienced adversity actually provides a new point of reference for our lives and can enlarge our ministry.

Suffering also affords us the opportunity to identify with Jesus. In Philippians 3:10 Paul stated, *I want to know Christ and the power of his resurrection and the fellowship of sharing in his sufferings, becoming like him in his death.* In addition to associating with Christ through other means, Paul desired to identify intimately with Christ through the fellowship of personal suffering. Some believers desire to identify with only a partial list of qualities associated with the life of Jesus, remaining isolated from His undeserved persecution, suffering, and ridicule. Yet, these are some of the very situations that enable us to best identify with Jesus.

In addition, suffering produces perseverance, godly character, and greater hope within us. In Romans 5:3–5 Paul wrote, *We also rejoice in our sufferings, because we know that suffering produces perseverance; perseverance, character; and character, hope. And hope does not disappoint us, because God has poured out his love into our hearts by the Holy Spirit, whom he has given us.* God used suffering to develop within Paul godly character rather than self-pity, as well as the ability to endure rather than succumb to despair.

As with every believer, suffering enables us to test our faith to see where our hope truly lies (2 Corinthians 1:8–11; Hebrews 6:19–20). Having our minds set on the benefits, rather than the cost of suffering, will enable us to be victorious in trials rather than to be defeated or disappointed.

In discipling others, advise them that God may not change circumstances to alleviate our suffering, but He does promise to help change our attitude in response to it. Also, God will never allow us to experience suffering one moment longer than is necessary to fulfill His purposes. Therefore, we should focus on Christ rather than the length or severity of each trial.

Since placing our hope in anything or anyone other than Jesus produces insecurity, encourage those you mentor to avoid misplacing their hope. Show them that as they consistently put their hope in Christ, He will renew their strength and enable them to rise above their circumstances (Isaiah 40:29–31). Because our caring God would never want us to suffer for the sake of suffering, encourage others to embrace trying times by choosing to rely on God's comfort and His ability to see them through.

Injustice

At times adversity arrives in the form of unfairness or injustice. Consider the life of Job: In the midst of great adversity, Job was mistreated and unjustly accused by those presumably closest to him.

Instead of being distracted by the trying situation, Job chose to draw ever closer to God, relying on His promises rather than on man (Job 16:20–21). Since God is bigger than any challenge we might face, the importance lies not with an unfair situation but with our response to it. Through trusting God, rather than the appearance of circumstances, we, like Job, can be confident that God will fulfill His purpose in us.

Instead of becoming offended by an injustice, practice responding with love, as Jesus did, when wronged. Choose to view the situation from God's perspective by seeking purpose rather than retribution. Use the experience as a learning tool, so that you will be careful to treat others rightly. Regardless of whether you experience injustice as a direct or indirect choice on the part of others, choosing to forgive will result in victory for you and honor for Christ.

Some people consider an apparent misfortune as unjust because they did nothing to contribute to the calamity. However, rather than judge an apparent misfortune by sight, we can look at it from a perspective of faith by relying on truth. For example, 1 Samuel 2:7 says, *The LORD sends poverty and wealth; he humbles and he exalts.* The truth is, everything that appears to belong to us has been given to us by God and actually belongs to Him. Therefore, the same God that withholds from us is the same God that bestows to us; we can trust His greater purpose in both giving and withholding.

Job 1:13–19 records that in one day Job lost all of his children, some of his servants, and all of his livestock. How did Job respond to such an apparently horrific injustice? Job 1:20–22 tells us, *At this, Job got up and tore his robe and shaved his head. Then he fell to the ground in worship and said: "Naked I came from my mother's womb, and naked I will depart. The LORD gave and the LORD has taken away; may the name of the LORD be praised." In all this, Job did not sin by charging God with wrongdoing.*

In the midst of suffering devastating loss, rather than charge God with misconduct, Job chose to praise and worship Him. How is this possible? Make no mistake. This would not be possible apart from the supernatural work of God. Job pursued God's will *in advance* of adversity. He was familiar with the character of God and knew He was in control of all things (Job 1:1–12). Even in the midst of tragedy, Job trusted God.

In discipling others, help them see that God uses unjust situations to develop our character and reliance on Him. He will also use what some may consider unfortunate circumstances to test and exercise our faith. Encourage others to allow the Lord to teach them to apply spiritual truths during these times, by focusing on God and His Word instead of on circumstances or self. In doing so, they will be spiritually victorious in every situation.

Persecution

As we watch the world news, many of us will never be able to grasp the extent to which some believers have been persecuted. Although some forms of persecution seem insignificant when compared to others, God wants us to realize that everyone who genuinely pursues Jesus will suffer some degree of persecution (2 Timothy 3:12). Since Jesus has nothing in common with the world, His followers shouldn't be surprised when they aren't embraced by those who live by the world's standards. Look at 1 Peter 4:12–13: *Dear friends, do not be surprised at the painful trial you are suffering, as though something strange were happening to you. But rejoice that you participate in the sufferings of Christ, so that you may be overjoyed when his glory is revealed.* Rather than be caught off guard, we are to practice rejoicing when persecuted for our faith, trusting God's glory will be revealed as we depend on His truth to see us through.

In discipling others, advise them that insults based on their faith are not directed at them personally but at Christ whom they represent. In Matthew 5:11-12 Jesus said, *"Blessed are you when people insult you, persecute you and falsely say all kinds of evil against you because of me. Rejoice and be glad, because great is your reward in heaven, for in the same way they persecuted the prophets who were before you."* Encourage others that being prepared and resolved to stand firm in Christ will provide victory in the midst of persecution.

Adversity by Design

In addition to God allowing adversity in our lives, there are also times when He will actually lead us into adversity. Exodus 13:17–18 provides us with such an example: *When Pharaoh let the people go, God did not lead them on the road through the Philistine country, though that was shorter. For God said, "If they face war, they might change their minds and return to Egypt." So God led the people around by the desert road toward the Red Sea.*

Our culture often views the easiest or fastest route as the best. However, rather than lead according to ease, the Lord guides in ways that build character and result in honoring Him. Therefore, we should examine each journey from God's perspective while considering possible lessons He wants to teach us. Each journey may not be easy, but we can experience peace by trusting that God's direction is best.

Sometimes God will lead us into challenging situations to test our character and faith. Deuteronomy 8:2 says, *Remember how the LORD your God led you all the way in the desert these forty years, to humble you and to test you in order to know what was in your heart, whether or not you would keep his commands.* Even though God may lead us into desert places, He will also triumphantly lead us through them. God will use adversity to reveal our spiritual condition, to humble us, and to rid us of self-reliance. Don't miss this: It is in times of adversity, rather than ease, that genuine faith is revealed. How well we respond in adversity will depend on how well we have prepared to be tested.

In discipling others, encourage them to embrace the truth that God may lead them into adversity. In the same way a classroom test reveals what a student believes to be true about a particular subject, real-life situations can test us and reveal what we believe to be true about God. In Job 23:10–12 the author wrote, *"But he knows the way that I take; when he has tested me, I will come forth as gold. My feet have closely followed his steps; I have kept to his way without turning aside. I have not departed from the commands of his lips; I have treasured the words of his mouth more than my daily bread."*

Job recognized his difficult circumstances as a test. Though he didn't always sense God's presence, he knew that God was near and faithful. Teach those you mentor that clinging to truth, especially in adverse situations, will prevent regret and reveal God's glory.

Spiritual Warfare

When one chooses to live for the Lord, they will often experience adversity stemming from spiritual warfare. Because the enemy would love to catch us unaware, spiritual warfare can begin subtly, develop quickly, and occur when we least expect it. For this reason, we are to be prepared in advance to face the challenge of spiritual conflict.

When the enemy comes against us, a battle line is drawn and two different sides are established. For disciples of Jesus, being on the correct side of any battle is to be innocent according to biblical truth. When we are consistently living according to truth, innocent of wrongdoing, such a battle or conflict is the Lord's. This means that we resist taking matters into our own hands while allowing God to contend with the opposition in His perfect way and timing. Psalm 35:1–3 says, *Contend, O LORD, with those who contend with me; fight against those who fight against me. Take up shield and buckler; arise and come to my aid. Brandish spear and javelin against those who pursue me. Say to my soul, "I am your salvation."* In challenging times such as these we are to rest in Christ, trusting Him to contend with those who contend with us.

In discipling others, encourage them to trust in Jesus in the midst of spiritual warfare by remaining focused on this truth: God is our refuge, He alone preserves our honor and integrity for His name's sake (Psalm 62:5–8). Show others how to diligently pursue God's guidance and counsel in the midst of spiritual warfare; and to walk in obedience, despite opposition. Remind them that advance training will aid in securing spiritual victory in times of battle.

Yet

We know that preparing ourselves with truth in advance of hardship will assist in preventing us from investing in anxious thoughts. Learning to use the word yet will aid in transitioning from thoughts and emotions that oppose God to those that reflect truth, enabling you to stand firm in the midst of adversity. For example, Psalm 42:5 begins with the author discouraged by adversity: *Why are you downcast, O my soul? Why so disturbed within me?* Then, he chooses to make a conscious effort to turn to truth. He says to himself: *Put your hope in God, for I will yet praise him, my Savior and my God.* The Psalmist's use of the word yet signifies a deliberate, personal choice to turn from a position of taking inventory of his emotions to one resting securely on truth.

Another example is found in Habakkuk 3:17–19: *Though the fig tree does not bud and there are no grapes on the vines, though the olive crop fails and the fields produce no food, though there are no sheep in the pen and no cattle in the stalls, yet I will rejoice in the LORD, I will be joyful in God my Savior. The Sovereign LORD is my strength; He makes my feet like the feet of a deer, he enables me to go on the heights.* Even though his initial words reflect potential despair, the prophet chose to remind himself of God's character and promises. By using the word yet we, too, can transition from personal feelings to thoughts of absolute truth, bringing hope to seemingly hopeless situations.

In discipling others, practice being sensitive to the adversity they are facing while encouraging them to use the word yet to transition to an active trust in truth. You may want to use Romans 8:35–39 to show that in adversity believers are more than conquerors. Then, explain that each experience of adversity comes with a choice: We can either choose to be overwhelmed or defeated, or trust the God of the universe to see us through. The one who chooses to trust will grow deeper in their faith and commitment to the Lord and, as a result, Jesus will receive the glory.

CHAPTER TWENTY-FOUR

Learning from Experience

God's deepest desire is for each of us to be proactive in our pursuit of righteousness. But He also knows that, because we're human, even our most sincere spiritual pursuits can be hampered by mistakes. Rather than being discouraged by errors, Jesus wants us to embrace them as opportunities for learning and training. Proverbs 3:11–12 says, *My son, do not despise the LORD's discipline and do not resent his rebuke, because the LORD disciplines those he loves, as a father the son he delights in.*

How precious that our Lord Jesus would care so deeply for our well-being that He would lovingly correct us! After all, mistakes in judgment or missteps in behavior are not nearly as significant as the necessity to learn from them. While the Holy Spirit works within us to correct misguided thinking and behavior, the enemy works diligently to remind us of and, possibly, falsely condemn us for personal wrongdoing. By giving into the enemy, we can easily become distracted and defeated rather than grow through personal mistakes. Therefore, we should develop a pattern of resisting the devil and relying on Christ to mature us spiritually through our life experiences.

Throughout each day, our actions are based on how we think. Consequently, spiritual mistakes often originate with errors in thought. In other words, missing the mark through personal behavior is often the result of believing incorrect information. By first identifying and acknowledging a particular undesired action or behavior, we can then further investigate to identify the point of error in thinking.

The desirability of an action or behavior can be determined by whether or not it pleases God. If a personal behavior draws us closer to Christ and honors Him, then it pleases God and is desirable. If our behavior fails to reflect Christ's nature or His Word, then it is undesirable. As believers longing to continually mature in Christ, it is imperative that we consistently invite the Lord Jesus to show us personal behaviors that fall short of reflecting His glory.

Unfortunately, merely learning to recognize and acknowledge undesired behavior will not correct it. Therefore, after identifying a behavior as undesirable, we are to then evaluate our personal thought process to determine where we missed the mark. This requires looking back to reexamine an occurrence, with the goal of learning from it to prevent future missteps (Lamentations 3:40).

Let's first practice identifying an undesired behavior. For example, let's say that a situation has resulted in you becoming worried. We know that the source of worry isn't the Lord because He instructs us in Matthew 6:25 not to worry. Also, since worry denies God's power, this would not be His desired outcome in any circumstance. We would be misrepresenting His character by doing so. In addition, worry distracts us, causing us to be ineffective for the work of Christ's kingdom. Therefore, worry is an undesired behavior and needs to be corrected.

Now let's consider the importance of reexamining the potential steps that can lead us to spend time in wrong thinking and eventual undesired behavior. Spiritual error occurs each time we give into a temptation to think or act contrary to truth. By reexamining a situation with the goal of learning from the experience, we are inviting the Holy Spirit to reveal to us specific temptations.

Let's use the previous example of worry to practice the application of these truths. After identifying worry as an undesired outcome, begin tracing both your actions and thought process backwards. While doing so, ask God to reveal any time that you may have invested in incorrect information. In the case of worry, using questions such as these can promote spiritually discerning thought patterns:

Did I see my circumstance and choose to rely on my limited perception of the situation rather than trust in what God could do? Did I focus on my inadequacies rather than the power of Almighty God? Did I allow what others were saying about the situation to affect my way of thinking?

In addition to pinpointing specific temptations, we should also review situations to determine where we may have missed avenues of escape or God's provision of a way out of temptation (1 Corinthians 10:13). For example, perhaps the Lord prompted you to end a conversation rather than allow a friend to tempt you with worrisome words. Maybe the Holy Spirit reminded you to meditate on His promises, yet you chose to invest in idle, anxious thinking.

Then, through awareness and reliance on the Spirit's power, we can become proactive in guarding against future, similar temptations, thereby learning from experience. Once you've identified your personal weakness in specific temptations, consistently ask the Lord to enable you to recognize future temptations and to guard your heart and mind against giving into them.

Another example might be that you find yourself confused by a situation. The Bible teaches that God is not a God of confusion (1 Corinthians 14:33). Therefore, confusion is not from the Lord and should be considered an undesired outcome. Choose to learn from the experience by asking yourself questions from a biblical perspective while inviting the Holy Spirit to pinpoint any error in judgment.

For instance, did I genuinely seek God's will in this matter, or did I pursue other avenues of guidance? Did I act on truth that God revealed to me through His Word and prayer, or did I follow the leading of an opposing source? Is the confusion coming from within my thoughts or from the conflicting perspective of another person's point of view? Practice enlisting the help of the Holy Spirit to assist you in recognizing errors in thinking, and then rely on His power to aid in correcting them. Then, ask the Lord to guard your heart and mind against future temptations.

In discipling others, you may find that people who are sincere in pursing righteousness are at times hard on themselves when they make mistakes. Hebrews 12:11 says, N*o discipline seems pleasant at the time, but painful. Later on, however, it produces a harvest of righteousness and peace for those who have been trained by it.* Lovingly remind others that training in righteousness is a process.

When a person solicits your help in working through a personal error, be quick to praise their willingness to correct mistakes. Teach them to identify and specifically acknowledge each undesired outcome, and to look back on situations to determine wrong thinking that produced such an outcome. Encourage others to continually learn from experience, noting that learning from error promotes spiritual maturity.

CHAPTERS 25 THROUGH 27

PURPOSEFUL MENTORING

CHAPTER TWENTY-FIVE

Recognizing and Seizing Godly Appointments

As you grow in your relationship with Jesus and become more comfortable in sharing His truth, you'll most likely grow increasingly sensitive to the lives around you. In addition to those people that God daily places in your life, He will also call you to a deeper commitment to other people and areas of service. For example, you may be invited to facilitate a weekly prayer group, teach a Bible study, or disciple a person one-on-one. How do you know whether to accept such invitations? While an open schedule signifies our availability, it fails to fully confirm God's call to accept what is proposed or offered. Since God's plans are always best for our lives, making a commitment should result from seeking His direction and receiving His approval.

In addition to people inviting you to areas of service, the Lord will also appoint you to such positions to further His kingdom (Romans 1:1). In other words, there will be occasions when God places on your heart a specific assignment or ministry He wants you to be involved in, without an invitation from others. In considering each appointment, we should faithfully follow Christ's lead.

We can recognize personal godly appointments as those that both align with biblical truth and have God's confirmation. As you seek His discernment in specific areas of service, God will sometimes confirm His will through other people or circumstances and will always confirm it through His provision of abiding peace (1 Corinthians 14:33). If you're not experiencing Christ's peace, it's a strong indicator that you should wait rather than accept a position of service. By committing to only those things God asks of us, we can approach them, confident God will accomplish His will.

As you contemplate godly appointments, remember service to Christ's kingdom involves people, not merely tasks. Consequently, God will purposefully place you in the lives of individuals to represent Him and teach them to apply His practical truth. Sometimes God will call us to sow, or plant, seeds of truth in the lives of nonbelievers. At other times, divine assignments may lead us to develop relationships with believers who need to be mentored or, perhaps, held accountable to live according to truth.

Discipleship through Planting and Watering

As we further examine these types of godly appointments, ask the Holy Spirit to reveal to you those people He has appointed for you to influence for His kingdom. For example, there may be times when the Lord guides you to invest in the lives of people who need to be introduced to biblical truth, or in others who need previously planted truth watered. These may be persons you interact with on a regular basis such as a neighbor, co-worker, or family member. They may not know who Jesus is, or may know about Him but haven't yet entered into a relationship with Him. They may or may not attend church. It's possible that these people are not familiar with the Bible or the significance God's Word holds for their lives. Therefore, the truth you share and the lifestyle you demonstrate are of utmost importance.

These people have been placed in your life to provide them with an understanding and, perhaps, even an introduction to the truth of Jesus Christ. In some instances, the adage, "You may be the only Jesus a person sees" could be true. Are there any people currently in your life who fit this description?

Colossians 4:5–6 tells us, *Be wise in the way you act toward outsiders; make the most of every opportunity. Let your conversation be always full of grace, seasoned with salt, so that you may know how to answer everyone.* We make the most of every opportunity by being prepared to speak truth to those God has placed within our sphere of influence and by praying for and anticipating the Lord providing such occasions. As we strive to influence the lost for Christ, we are to be wise, relying on God's supernatural discernment, powerful Word, and enablement. Since salt, or truth, is a preservative, choosing to sprinkle it graciously throughout our conversations will provide potential preservation of those who are separated from Jesus.

Discipleship through Mentoring

In addition to planting and watering seeds of truth in nonbelievers, God will also place in your life believers that He wants you to mentor. To mentor or disciple a believer is to encourage, teach, guide, and train an individual according to biblical truth with the purpose of developing spiritual maturity. As a result, they can reproduce truth in the lives of others. Whether a person considers themselves to be young or old in the faith, those seeking genuine discipleship training desire to develop a deeper relationship with Jesus. They are usually at least somewhat familiar with Scripture, but may or may not engage in consistent Bible study or devote themselves to prayer.

Even though a person claims to know Jesus, he or she may struggle with their daily walk. You may also find that some people who believe they are saved and going to heaven don't understand how to live victoriously under the Lordship of Jesus Christ. Perhaps they've never been trained to do so. Praise God for you! You can be instrumental in training others to follow Christ completely, according to His perfect will and way.

Through intentionally spending quality time with a believer, teaching truth and demonstrating its practical application for daily living, you will be training them to be more like Jesus. Paul gave us a glimpse of this process in 1 Thessalonians 1:4–6: *For we know, brothers loved by God, that he has chosen you, because our gospel came to you not simply with words, but also with power, with the Holy Spirit and with deep conviction. You know how we lived among you for your sake. You became imitators of us and of the Lord.* Paul understood that true discipleship makes life the classroom. He chose to include others in his daily life for their spiritual well-being. Are you willing to regularly engage in people's daily lives for their spiritual benefit? Since a person can't walk in obedience to Jesus until they first understand what obedience looks like, individual discipleship provides enormous spiritual benefits.

So, how do you know when you're prepared to mentor someone through discipleship training? We just learned that to spiritually mentor someone is to teach them biblical truth by means of communication and example. Therefore, the life of a mentor should be well-grounded in God's Word and a consistent demonstration of biblical truth. In 1 Timothy 4:12, Paul encouraged Timothy to be an example of Christ to those entrusted to him: *Don't let anyone look down on you because you are young, but set an example for the believers in speech, in life, in love, in faith and in purity.*

Paul wasn't concerned with whether Timothy met the expectations of others, but that his lifestyle met God's expectations. In doing so, Timothy would be setting an accurate example for others to follow. Are you surrendered and committed to obeying God's will in assisting others in their spiritual walk with Jesus?

It's beneficial to recognize that the potential to train fellow believers in godliness is always present, whether they realize it or not. This means that the Lord may give you opportunities to teach believers in subtle ways, promoting growth in their trust and reliance on Christ. For example, it may be that a co-worker will ask you for biblical insight concerning an on-going family matter. Maybe a neighbor will periodically ask you to help them recognize God's perspective in matters of parenting. Since Jesus has commissioned each of His followers to teach others to obey all His instructions, be continually prayerful, prepared, and anticipating teachable moments with fellow believers.

In addition to informal opportunities, God will also provide you with formal opportunities to train believers to more fully depend on Him. As those around you become aware of Jesus' power at work in your life, you may be approached by people asking you to mentor them or others they know. A person may, for example, approach you to disciple them personally. A parent may ask you to mentor their child, or a minister might solicit you to disciple a new believer. The following will assist you in determining God's best appointments for one-on-one mentoring.

As with other potential appointments, the opportunity to mentor someone should be brought to the Lord in prayer, allowing Him to reveal His will. Even though you may be an effective mentor and someone communicates a need to be mentored, you may not be the one called by God to do so. For instance, a person will be incapable of leading someone beyond their own level of spiritual maturity. Therefore, a mentor is to demonstrate more spiritual wisdom and maturity than those they disciple.

There may be other considerations guiding your personal commitment to disciple another. For instance, there may be occasions when the person asking to be mentored is a relative, friend, or close friend of your family. Although this doesn't make it impossible for you to become their mentor, the person may have failed to consider that sharing openly and honestly with you could be difficult. Because an effective mentoring relationship is based on these elements, ask the person to consider whether they can be transparent in discussing personal topics with you, as they pertain to truth. If not, graciously show them that this would limit their success and direct them to prayerfully consider other possible mentors.

In trying to ascertain whether or not you are to mentor someone it's also worthwhile to explore the person's expectations. You can't give someone the desire to walk in obedience to truth, nor can you make them teachable. Therefore, despite your sincerity, you may not be able to meet some of their expectations. For this reason, when approached by someone on the subject of mentoring, ask the following questions. "What are your expectations for the mentoring process?" Or, "What did you have in mind when you considered individual discipleship?"

The response to these questions will often reveal a person's expectations. For example, a parent asking you to mentor their child may respond, "I can't get my teen to obey me; I thought if they had a mentor it might help." Or, "I don't know much about the Bible, but I want my child to know more." These types of answers reveal a desire on the part of the parent, but not on the part of the child. In these instances you may want to ask further questions to determine the child's expectations and whether or not a mentor is the correct solution. Also, ask the parent to pray concerning God's desired role for you in the life of their child.

On the other hand, a parent may respond to the initial question with something like, "My teen desires to grow in their understanding of the Bible; but I'm not sure I can take them very far, or that I would be the best one to do that." In seeking God's wisdom and discernment, He may lead you to meet personally with the child before committing to mentor them. Furthermore, God may lead you to engage the parent in a conversation about their own personal discipleship. As you do, be open to the Lord's direction and then obediently follow His will.

Sometimes questioning a person who is seeking personal discipleship will reveal their desire for a quick solution to an immediate problem, or a need for assistance in gaining closure to a current situation. In either case, point the person to applicable Scripture for their situation. Then, wait to see if the person is content with the information provided to them, or if they continue to show further interest in being mentored.

At times people may ask about discipleship because they're not familiar with the idea, purpose, or benefits of this training. In addition to helping a person consider the significance of personal discipleship, you may also be led to have them weigh the cost as Jesus did in Luke 14:28–33: "*Suppose one of you wants to build a tower. Will he not first sit down and estimate the cost to see if he has enough money to complete it? For if he lays the foundation and is not able to finish it, everyone who sees it will ridicule him, saying, 'This fellow began to build and was not able to finish.'*

Or suppose a king is about to go to war against another king. Will he not first sit down and consider whether he is able with ten thousand men to oppose the one coming against him with twenty thousand? If he is not able, he will send a delegation while the other is still a long way off and will ask for terms of peace. In the same way, any of you who does not give up everything he has cannot be my disciple."

Since Christ requires full surrender in the lives of His followers, it's very important for those inquiring about discipleship to grasp this truth. After explaining the cost of discipleship, the person may decline or want time to further consider their decision. In this situation, lovingly ask the person to take their concerns to Jesus. Then, pray that the Lord will draw the person closer to Himself.

There may be occasions when the Holy Spirit directs you to invite an individual to be mentored, making personal discipleship training available to them. In this instance, it would be advantageous for you to seek the Lord's timing in the invitation and to allow the person to prayerfully consider the offer. Regardless of the means by which an opportunity to mentor someone occurs, as Jesus' disciples, we are to be diligent in following God's lead while leaving the results to Him.

In contemplating mentoring others in discipleship, it's equally important to be mindful of those things that do not define a spiritual mentor. For example, a mentor is not a lending institution, a licensed social worker, or child care provider. Even so, God certainly places people in our lives for us to meet a multitude of needs. So, how do you know what lines to draw or boundaries to establish with those you mentor?

Let's suppose God has placed in your life a person who is experiencing financial hardship. As you seek God's wisdom in this situation, He prompts you to use pertinent Scripture to encourage the person to view their situation from His perspective and to trust Christ to meet their needs. Then, encourage them to take each specific need to God in prayer, leaving it in His care. As you pray for them, ask the Lord to use this time to stretch their faith and bring honor to Him. Also, ask God to show you anything He wants you to do in this situation, and trust Him to enable you to do it.

So, what should you do if the person asks you for money? After all, the Bible teaches us to give to those who are in need (Proverbs 19:17; Romans 12:13). As in each scenario, it would be wise to be prayerfully prepared. This doesn't mean that you won't be prompted by the Lord to financially help this person. But it does mean that your actions should reflect God's will rather than your own. Abiding in Jesus will prevent acting merely on emotion, out of obligation, or because the situation makes you uncomfortable.

Since God's ways are higher than ours, we don't always have a full understanding of what He is doing. If we get in the way of His work, we risk jeopardizing all He might otherwise accomplish. Perhaps, in the case of the person asking for money, God wants to use this circumstance to train them to grow in deeper dependence on Him. If you automatically give them money, you would be postponing the very spiritual lesson God wants to teach them.

Jesus teaches us to stand firm on the decisions we make that are based on the truth of God's Word and the leading of His Spirit. As a result, we can confidently live by personal decisions that clearly reflect God's truth and His will. This type of lifestyle is not only pleasing to God but also leaves little room for regret that often results from moving in our own direction or in our own strength. Almighty God meets each and every need as He sees fit. Therefore, we should also be sensitive to the fact that the direction God leads in one situation may not be the way He guides in a different, yet similar, circumstance. Once again, we see a need for continuous reliance on Christ for discernment and wisdom, especially in mentoring others.

In further considering those qualifications that do not define a spiritual mentor, be aware that a mentor is not a professional counselor. Therefore, we should be prepared to recognize situations or possible behaviors that may require professional, qualified expertise. For example, caution should be used with behaviors or conversations that reflect potential psychosis, depression, demonic strongholds, self-harming or suicidal tendencies, addictions to alcohol or drugs, eating disorders, and experiences of physical, emotional, or sexual abuse. Since you may not know an individual's experiences or needs, it's valuable to have in mind a trustworthy professional you can refer people to. Since victory can only be found in Jesus Christ, be conscientious to choose a professional who will use godly principles to guide and equip people.

Discipleship through Accountability

As you teach others to walk in obedience to God's instructions, the Lord will purposefully place in your life those whom He wants you to hold spiritually accountable to live according to truth. Since we can't expect those who don't know Jesus to reflect Him, those persons you would be holding accountable have demonstrated evidence of a personal relationship with Christ. These people acknowledge the Bible as their personal standard for living and are striving to be more like Jesus.

As with all other areas of discipleship, holding a fellow believer accountable should be done in love, with the correct heart motive, and by the guidance and authority of the Holy Spirit. Therefore, when holding others accountable for personal choices and behavior, we are to rely on the Holy Spirit by approaching them in His timing and in the manner He shows us. Then, follow up by praying that each person will allow God to do a thorough work in their hearts and lives. It's also important to realize that a person can only truly hold someone accountable who chooses to receive accountability. For this reason, carefully follow what the Lord shows you to do and leave the results to Him. The one who genuinely desires to be obedient to Christ will accept loving correction (Galatians 6:1–2).

Because our Holy God has high expectations for His disciples (1 Peter 1:16), we should have high expectations for fellow believers. Accountability is a key tool in striving to meet such expectations. How are you valuing accountability in your life and in the lives of fellow believers?

God has a strategy for furthering His kingdom and desires for you to be a specific part of it. Be aware that godly callings are often outside the church walls. As you become a living example of Jesus' character and His Word, everywhere you go has the potential for structured and unstructured discipleship training. Because you cannot be in two places at one time, begin to develop the habit of faithfully relying on God's wisdom and discernment to recognize godly appointments. Then choose to trust in His ability to accomplish His eternal purpose in each assignment.

CHAPTER TWENTY-SIX

Plan to Succeed

So far, we've discussed various ways for you to equip yourself to be successful in personal discipleship and ways to prepare to disciple others. We will now review a practical plan to begin effectively mentoring on an individual basis. As with any endeavor in life, a person will fail to experience long-term success without a plan. The same can be true in making disciples.

To become familiar with any plan is to allow it to become commonplace in our lives. God's plan to reproduce disciples is based on believers teaching others to obey everything He commands through personal and practical application of the Bible. They, in turn, will watch our lives closely to see what it looks like to walk in obedience. As His plan for applying truth develops into a lifestyle, you will become increasingly comfortable and confident in discipleship. Also, you'll experience greater effectiveness in teaching from a position of personal experience rather than merely from theory.

For this to take place, you'll need to gain knowledge and experience.

Diligently study the Scriptures provided in this book in order to gain personal knowledge of the Bible and how it specifically applies to your life. Then, acquire valuable experience by establishing and consistently practicing its foundational principles. As a result, you'll be better prepared to effectively train others in one-on-one discipleship.

The role of mentoring or discipling individuals is different from facilitating or teaching group Bible studies. There are some similarities, since group Bible studies can assist in successfully developing personal knowledge and understanding of the Bible. However, within a group, it's often difficult to ascertain whether each individual is grasping the biblical principles being taught and implementing them correctly in their daily lives.

Spiritual, one-on-one training enables a person to examine God's Word as it specifically pertains to their life. A mentor can then encourage them to consider personal application of biblical principles, challenging the person to practice each principle throughout the day. In addition, a person being spiritually mentored accepts personal responsibility and accountability to mature in their relationship with Jesus. This makes individual discipleship an effective means to fulfill our commission to teach others to obey everything God commands.

Although a group Bible study may go on for an extended period of time, in most cases, it should take only a matter of weeks to train a believer to pursue righteousness for themselves. Therefore, it's beneficial to set a time frame for individual discipleship. Initially, ask the person desiring to be mentored to commit to meet once a week at an appointed time. Although there may be occasions when you both need to be flexible, scheduling regular meetings provides accountability to the commitment made to the process. The number of meetings can vary due to such issues as spiritual maturity, learning style, or unforeseen circumstances. Ten to eleven weeks is typically sufficient time to mentor someone. As you become more comfortable with mentoring others, you'll be able to better discern the number of meetings that are needed. In addition to scheduling an initial ten-week commitment, I tell each person that the exact length of time needed to complete training will be determined as we spend more time together.

Since a mentor represents Christ, it is important to be on time. I personally set the length of each meeting at about one hour, while being continuously sensitive to the leading of the Holy Spirit. This means that there may be times the Spirit leads you to finish early or shows you that more time is necessary for the work He is achieving.

Because God is a god of detail, we should also consider His best in selecting a place to meet. The location should be free from noise and distractions. For example, if you open your home or choose to meet in the person's home you disciple, previous arrangements should be made to care for children or pets. In considering a public place, be sure it offers a specific area where you will be uninterrupted. Commit each detail to the Lord and faithfully follow His directives.

After committing to disciple an individual, but before beginning the first training session, you may find it beneficial to ask the person to share their spiritual history. This can be achieved by asking questions like, "Would you tell me a little about your spiritual journey?" Or, "Could you give me some insight into where you believe you are spiritually?" The person's response may provide insight into their spiritual needs, reveal specific ways to be praying for them, and aid in determining the direction to take in training. You may also ask if they desire any specific topics to be covered during your time together.

Bear in mind that the amount of knowledge a person learns and comprehends can depend on the method by which they are taught. Since people learn in a variety of ways, it's also valuable to take into account each individual's needs in order to be most effective. After all, the best trainer is not one who asks others to adapt to their methods of training, but instead adapts their training methods to best fit the learning style of those being taught. For this reason, be continually open and willing to allow God to mold you into the trainer, or mentor, He desires you to be.

Psalm 119:73 says, *Your hands made me and formed me; give me understanding to learn your commands.* Since each individual is uniquely created by God, ask Him to give you insight into the learning style that is unique to each person you disciple. Considering the following questions may be helpful: Is it easy for the person to learn by listening to instruction? Do they have a visual learning style, comprehending more effectively from written directions, images, or objects? Is it helpful for the person to understand an overall concept before receiving details concerning the same concept? Do they benefit from the explanation of the smaller details of a principle in order to see the bigger picture? Are they an analytical thinker? Do they appreciate word pictures? Throughout the discipleship process, ask the Holy Spirit to show you creative ways to teach each individual how to apply truth.

Then prayerfully continue to commit your work to the Lord. Ask God to provide you with wisdom and discernment to best meet the spiritual needs of those you disciple. Ask Him to prepare you and equip you in every way, enabling you to be sensitive and obedient to His leading. Throughout your training, pray that God will create within the heart of the person you are mentoring a teachable spirit and a desire to pursue righteousness. Ask Him to protect your time together and to eliminate any obstacles or distractions that may prevent them from hearing truth and surrendering to it. Continually commit your efforts to the Lord and leave the results to Him.

As God shows you those He would have you personally mentor, be faithful to your place of service, acknowledging it as His appointment (John 15:16). Remember, part of God's plan in mentoring others is to train them to depend solely on Jesus and His Word rather than on you. In doing so, they will become spiritually self-disciplined in obeying God's commands.

CHAPTER TWENTY-SEVEN

The Process of Mentoring

As you equip yourself with the necessary tools of discipleship, you are setting the stage to begin mentoring individuals. Once you're prepared, all that is left is for you to begin. This chapter will explain in practical terms how to actually begin mentoring an individual, show you what a first mentoring session might look like, and help you consider what may comprise future training sessions.

After greeting the person you're mentoring, begin each week's mentoring session with prayer. Doing so not only demonstrates the priority of prayer in your own life, but also trains others to maintain focus on the Lord. This practice will also assist in preventing prolonged socializing and will help to effectively transition into the week's training. Including specific prayers for the person you're mentoring will encourage them to anticipate God working on their behalf. For instance, ask the Holy Spirit to prevent them from being distracted and to give them full understanding of the truth being presented.

Also, be committed to closing your time together in prayer, conveying the importance of asking God to accomplish His work in this person's life. As you pray for God's will to be done, you'll be training them to further consider God's best for their life, depend more fully on Jesus, and anticipate His powerful work. In addition, your example will be teaching them to consider ways they can specifically pray for their own needs and those of others.

Expectations for Purposeful Mentoring

After opening in prayer, use the beginning of your first training session to provide the person with basic guidelines for your time together. For example, you can encourage them by explaining that you've been praying for them, and are anticipating Christ doing a mighty work in their life. Since a person will struggle to effectively apply truth in their life until they first grasp it, invite them to stop you, whenever necessary, to ask questions or to gain better understanding.

Then, using Scripture, begin communicating what Jesus expects to achieve in the lives of His disciples and how you intend to assist in that endeavor.

1. Read together Matthew 28:18–20.

Explain that God has expectations and a plan for each of us to enter into and to mature in a personal relationship with Him. This process includes learning how to walk in faithful obedience to the Lord's instructions as well as teaching others.

To help a person understand this process, it may be worthwhile to ask them to consider how they learned to write their name or ride a bike. Just being taught to do these things wasn't enough; they had to receive the teaching and put it into practice in order to really learn these skills. Explain that we mature in Christ as we are both taught and learn how to obey all of His instructions. This means that if what is being taught reflects God's truth, it isn't enough to merely acquire knowledge from the teaching. It must be put into practice to achieve lasting results. This may seem like a simple point but, sadly, many people who claim to know Jesus continue to listen to truth without practicing it. Consequently, the significance of walking in truth, rather than merely reading or talking about it, cannot be overstated.

With this in mind, invite the person you're mentoring to hold you accountable for linking each practical instruction to biblical truth. In doing so, you'll help them recognize the connection between truth and personal application. As their mentor, explain that you'll encourage, train, and hold them accountable to implement each biblical principle. Also, use Matthew 28:18–20 to show them that as they learn to obey God's commands, they can then make disciples by teaching others in the same manner. This reproduction of truth in the lives of others fulfills God's plan for disciple making.

It can be encouraging for the person you are mentoring to know that God wants His children to be successful. However, God's definition of success is much different from that of the world.

2. Read together Joshua 1:8.

"Do not let this Book of the Law depart from your mouth; meditate on it day and night, so that you may be careful to do everything written in it. Then you will be prosperous and successful." As a person intentionally takes the words of the Bible and applies them in daily life, they will

experience spiritual transformation or success. Train others to recognize that each spiritual journey is uniquely individual. For this reason, spiritual success is to be measured by God's standard, rather than the world's or through comparing oneself to others (2 Corinthians 10:12).

3. Read together 1 Timothy 4:7–8.

Have nothing to do with godless myths and old wives' tales; rather, train yourself to be godly. For physical training is of some value, but godliness has value for all things, holding promise for both the present life and the life to come. Then, explain that enormous benefits result from physical training. However, as we all know, there are no shortcuts to physical wellness. It requires determination, discipline, and correct choices to consistently eat right and exercise. This verse tells us that, although the benefits of physical training are valuable, the benefits of training in godliness are unlimited and eternal. Therefore, they are to be more highly regarded.

Although some people would rather invest in fad diets and weight loss pills to become physically fit, proper nutrition and exercise are the proven methods to achieve physical wellness. In the same way, those desiring to grow in godliness may pursue a variety of ways to do so. However, God develops spiritual wellness in us as we learn to abide with Jesus through daily Bible study and prayer. Again we can see that this process of gaining spiritual maturity involves consistent practice, requiring us to "train" ourselves.

Then, reread verse 7. Explain that training in godliness begins by abandoning all myths or tales that are contrary to biblical truth, clearing the way to invest deeply in the absolute truth of God's Word. Regardless of age, believers in Jesus should consistently be training themselves in godliness. Then, express this goal for your time together:

to equip them with basic Bible study and application skills, so that when your time together is finished they can then continue to train themselves in godliness.

Discipleship: A Process, Not a Program

Throughout the mentoring process, keep in mind that discipleship is *not* a program. Each individual is uniquely created by God with different personalities, learning styles, and life experiences. Rather than asking us to follow a program or predetermined schedule, God gave us His Word and made it applicable for all circumstances and situations in life. He desires for us to rely on His Word and the leading of His Spirit to reveal truth as it applies in the lives of those we mentor. Consequently you will find that through the process of discipling others, you, too, will grow increasingly dependent on the Lord and His Word.

God wants to do a thorough, rather than a partial or incomplete, work in the lives of His followers. Therefore, our goal should never be to have a set agenda or plan to cover as much material as possible in each session. Our goal in discipleship is to teach individuals to develop thought and behavior patterns based on truth and, as needed, to correct wrong thinking. This means that while we are being proactive in teaching biblical principles, it may also become necessary to help them correct thought patterns that oppose truth. Be watchful: If a person communicates thoughts or demonstrates actions that oppose God's Word or His character, it may indicate that they lack full understanding of a biblical principle, or have thought patterns that fail to line up with Scripture.

Let's consider, for instance, that the person you're mentoring reveals that they consistently experience fear. Since God wants us to have victory over fear, it's worthwhile to immediately address this issue, even though you may be prepared to cover it in the future. In such a case, the Lord may lead you to point them to Scripture about how to obtain victory over fear, and then interweave additional truths concerning the subject into future lessons.

In another example, the person you're mentoring tells you that, when young, they weren't taught about Jesus and have lingering resentment toward their parents for failing to provide a church experience. Hearing that they resent their parents, for whatever reason, could indicate hurt, bitterness, and unforgiveness. Because it will be difficult to walk in victory until fully dealing with their past, prayerfully consider training them in ways to settle their past as discussed in chapter 3. In each case, ask the Lord to guide and direct your steps and then faithfully follow His lead.

To be most effective in discipleship training, we are to consistently rely on the Holy Spirit to provide us with insight into an individual's spiritual maturity and needs. Then, using Scripture, assist the person in consistently identifying and implementing the next step of obedience. As we've discussed, this book is designed to equip you with many different tools to address a wide variety of spiritual issues. But not all issues will need to be addressed with each individual.

For instance, it may be that the person you are mentoring is proficient in studying the Bible, but has difficulty converting knowledge into practical application. In this case, it may not be necessary to spend much time teaching them ways to study the Bible, but it may be valuable to study various methods for applying it. In each case, become thoroughly familiar with the biblical tools for discipleship training as presented in this book. Then, rely on the Holy Spirit to direct each week's teaching according to the needs of the individual.

Although there may be times when the subject matter you're teaching could be considered basic, Christ-followers are only as strong as their understanding and application of foundational biblical principles. For this reason, avoid assuming that a person has previous comprehension of biblical truth. Even though a person may communicate knowledge of a particular principle, your job is to lovingly confirm that they have genuine application of it in their life.

Also, be mindful that the truth you've learned to walk in may be totally new to others. This should motivate you to be thorough, yet patient, in your instruction. Teach as God leads. Then, prior to moving on to another subject, ask Him to enable you to discern whether or not the person you are mentoring is successfully grasping each spiritual truth. Evaluating a person's responses to questions such as these will help in determining correct and complete comprehension: What do you understand this truth to mean? What do you think the Bible is saying here? Then, use interactive dialogue to confirm accurate understanding and to correct any misunderstanding.

Asking questions similar to the following will also help the person consider application of each principle: What difference should knowledge of this truth make in your life? What would you consider to be some practical ways to practice this particular Scripture? Moreover, evaluating choices and behavior will aid in verifying application of truth.

As you prepare for each week's discipleship training, keep in mind that God is a god of order. Therefore, be careful to present fundamental truths in correct order to prepare a foundation for the teaching of future principles. For example, a person will struggle to apply Scripture if they fail to first become yielded to following it. For this reason, teaching people to surrender to Christ by consistently yielding to His will should take precedence over teaching application of truth in relationships.

Since many biblical truths build upon one another, it may be necessary to review a particular principle, or to show the significant link between two biblical precepts before transitioning to another. Don't hesitate to take the time to do so. Our human nature desires to see progress in personal endeavors; discipleship training is no exception. However (and this is a big however), we must be continually reliant on the Lord to show us when to slow down, review, or even back up, rather than move forward in training.

Even though you'll be prepared each session to share specific truth, the person you are mentoring may arrive with other issues on their heart that require attention. Sometimes their comments or questions may lead in a direction other than the one you have prepared for. For example, you may be ready to teach on the subject of lordship when the person you're mentoring shares that their mother has just been diagnosed with cancer. It might be that while you're talking about sanctification the person begins asking what the Bible says about the subject of purity. These occasions can provide wonderful opportunities for people to see how application of truth can be lived out in real-life situations. Rather than becoming rattled or anxious, be sensitive to the Holy Spirit's guidance and trust He knows best. Ask the Lord to show you what to say, and then allow Him to lead your conversation in His desired direction.

Since mentoring is a process of both teaching and learning through application, a mentor should also be sensitive to a person's point of saturation. It's wise to stop at this point (when a person has taken in as much information as they are able to process) and allow adequate time to implement what was taught before teaching new subject matter. Also, it can be valuable to allow the person you're mentoring opportunity to ask questions between training sessions and prior to beginning each new session. Offering your e-mail address and phone number will give them access to not only ask questions but also to submit prayer requests between meetings.

Below is an outline and general description of the essential fundamentals of discipleship included in this book. Each chapter will help train you to walk in personal obedience to the Lord and teach others to do the same. If all subjects were discussed in your training time together, an eleven-week outline would look similar to the one below. I cannot express enough that discipleship is not a program. This means that each weekly training should be based on the guidance and leading of the Holy Spirit.

Because the work is His, closely following the leading and guidance of Christ Jesus will provide confidence in God's best plan for each person and will result in effective discipleship. It may be that God guides you to convey some subjects using fewer Scriptures or additional verses than those provided in this book, or to cover subjects not mentioned here. As you move forward through the process of discipleship training with each individual, remember to be flexible and obedient to the leading of God's Spirit in determining topics and length of study.

Although the explanation of Scripture found in this book may serve to be helpful in the process of making disciples, God alone knows the individual needs and makeup of each of His children. Therefore, before ending your training sessions together, ask Him to reveal any additional truths He would like you to share with the person you are discipling. You may also want to ask them if there is an additional subject they would like to cover.

As your training sessions come to a close, encourage the person to continue to train themselves in godliness through personal study and application of God's Word. Also, encourage them to consistently place themselves under sound biblical teaching and accountability to truth.

Week 1

Expectations for Purposeful Mentoring (Chapter 27)

Promoting Spiritual Growth (Chapter 10)

Teachability (Chapter 11)

Week 2

A Call to Surrender (Chapter 12)

Sanctification (Chapter 13)

Week 3

The Significance of Faith (Chapter 14)

Week 4

The Significance of Applying Truth (Chapter 15)

The Power Source (Chapter 16)

Week 5

How to Study the Bible for Application (Chapter 17)

Week 6

Applying Truth to Develop Identity in Christ (Chapter 18)

Week 7

Applying Truth to Fulfill God's Purpose (Chapter 19)

Week 8

Applying Truth to Correct Sin and Prevent Future Disobedience (Chapter 20)

Week 9

Applying Truth in Choices and Consequences (Chapter 21)

Week 10

Applying Truth in Relationships (Chapter 22)

Week 11

Applying Truth in Adversity (Chapter 23)

Learning from Experience (Chapter 24)

Personal Responsibility for Obedience

Even though God calls us to teach others to obey everything He has commanded, we cannot choose obedience for others. We are to pursue carefully only what Jesus asks of us and faithfully pray for each person's obedient response.

There may be occasions when the person you are mentoring begins to show signs or symptoms of not being fully committed to the discipleship process. Perhaps they are inconsistent in attendance, cancel rather than reschedule sessions, or desire to completely cancel future training. The person may meet with you each week, but they fail to demonstrate application of the truth being taught. Commit each situation to prayer rather than being discouraged. Keep in mind that a genuine, thorough, transforming work is produced by God and God alone. Therefore, if the person declines to finish training, commit to pray that God will give them the desire to wholeheartedly pursue Jesus.

Also, it would be unbeneficial for a person to go through the motions of discipleship only to communicate that spiritual training had no lasting effect. In such cases where the person you are mentoring is attending the training but not responding through application of truth, it may be that God would lead you to discontinue a mentoring relationship. Ask the Lord how to approach the person each week and whether He is calling you to remain committed to disciple them. Since it is never our goal to cause others to stumble, communicate, in love, the reason God may have you discontinue meeting together in advance of doing so. (This places the responsibility and accountability on the one being mentored.)

Remember, when mentoring others, we're simply promoting spiritual growth. Our responsibility lies in earnestly following God's lead, conveying His truth in love, and trusting Him for the results. Because all spiritual growth is the work of Almighty God, we should avoid taking responsibility for the outcome whether it appears positive or negative.

Be Encouraged

How wonderful that Jesus does not ask us to become disciples or to make disciples of others on our own, but assures us that He will be with us every step of the way (Matthew 28:20)! If at any time you experience doubt concerning your personal discipleship or your ability to make disciples of others, remember that apart from Christ, we can accomplish nothing (John 15:5), but with Him nothing is impossible (Luke 1:37).

Be encouraged that God has immediate and future purpose for your life. Rather than choosing to be overwhelmed by the task at hand, my prayer is that you will become filled with the love of Jesus and equipped with His truth. Be expectant of all God will accomplish in and through you as you choose to be intentional and purposeful in participating in His plan to make disciples.

APPENDIX

The History of God's Plan of Salvation

In the Old Testament, God made a covenant with His people, the Israelites, which included instructions about how to live in the way that was pleasing and obedient to Him (Exodus 20:1–17; 24:3–8). When people enter into a covenant, both sides usually have the opportunity to stipulate conditions of the agreement. However, in a covenant made between God and people, God sets the terms of the agreement and requires a response of obedience. God's designated penalty for disobedience, or sin, is death. (Ezekiel 18:20; Romans 6:23).

Throughout the Old Testament, our loving God provided a way for His people to atone for their sins through blood sacrifice. In Leviticus 17:11 God said, "'*For the life of a creature is in the blood, and I have given it to you to make atonement for yourselves on the altar; it is the blood that makes atonement for one's life.*'" God did not intend for these sacrifices to be a permanent solution for the atonement of sins.

Therefore, they had to be constantly repeated by His people. God's Old Testament covenant was broken as a result of the people's inability to accomplish a complete work through sacrifice.

Then, through the prophet Jeremiah and others, the Lord foretold of a new covenant with His people (Jeremiah 31:31–34). While the old covenant was not able to fully clear the conscience of sin and guilt, the new covenant, through the blood of Christ Jesus, would cleanse it from all unrighteousness (Hebrews 9:1–15). In other words, the old covenant was a symbolic, temporary, outer work of the complete, eternal, inner work that the new covenant would accomplish.

Jesus is the only one who could fully atone for sin. He is the only one perfect in every way, completely without sin (1 Peter 1:18–19). Although each of us most likely know some wonderful people, none of them are perfect. John the Baptist identified Jesus as the perfect sacrificial lamb in John 1:29: *The next day John saw Jesus coming toward him and said, "Look, the Lamb of God, who takes away the sin of the world!"* Today, we, too, should help others to recognize the truth of Jesus by proclaiming the good news of His atonement for sin.

Words Used in Sharing the Gospel

As you communicate the gospel message, the people you influence may not be familiar with the meanings of words used in Scripture. Therefore, it will be beneficial for you to study the following definitions and strive to memorize their meaning.

Grace: God's undeserved, unmerited favor. The benefits of grace include God's supernatural, enabling power.

Faith: Being certain or confident in the things of God regardless of whether they are visible. Faith has its origin in Jesus and is further developed through a growing relationship with Him.

Justification: Because God is just, He can't allow sin to go unpunished. God's appointed penalty for sin is separation from Him—death. Jesus paid the penalty in full so that those who believe in Him can be justified—restored to a relationship with God, free from sin and guilt.

Redemption: The means by which a person is justified. Jesus' sacrificial death on the cross paid the enormous penalty for our sin. That payment was exchanged for our penalty of sin, redeeming us from eternal sin and death. Redemption did not cancel our debt, but enabled it to be paid in full.

Reconciliation: Since sin opposes our holy God, living in sin separates us from Him. While sin made us enemies of God, belief in His Son and receiving His grace pardons us from sin, allowing us to be reconciled—united with Christ.

Bible Verses to Use in Sharing the Gospel

The verses below are by no means an exhaustive list of Bible passages that pertain to the gospel. They are merely a simple, practical guide to begin helping someone understand the gospel of God's grace.

Romans 5:8: *But God demonstrated his own love for us in this: While we were still sinners, Christ died for us.* Jesus' love for us is not dependent on our love for Him. Knowing full well that each of us is sinful and undeserving of His love, Christ gave His life on the cross for each of us.

Romans 6:23: *For the wages of sin is death, but the gift of God is eternal* *life in Christ Jesus our Lord.* Our holy God determined the penalty for sin to be death and permanent separation from Him. He also provided a means of escaping this penalty through belief in His Son, Jesus.

Romans 3:20: *Therefore no one will be declared righteous in his sight by observing the law; rather, through the law we become conscious of sin.* God's law makes each of us aware of what is right and wrong. However, there is no one capable of keeping the Law.

Romans 3:21–24: *But now a righteousness from God, apart from law, has been made known, to which the Law and the Prophets testify. This righteousness from God comes through faith in Jesus Christ to all who believe. There is no difference, for all have sinned and fall short of the glory of God, and are justified freely by his grace, through the redemption that came by Christ Jesus.* Everyone sins. Because God is without sin, each of us fall far short of His glorious nature. However, God provides the free gift of redemption. Through Jesus' sacrificial death on the cross we can be redeemed, or saved, from the penalty of sin. We are justified and brought into a right standing with God through His gift of unmerited favor, grace. Salvation cannot be earned or purchased; it is a free gift given to those who repent and believe.

Romans 10:9–10: *That if you confess with your mouth, "Jesus is Lord," and believe in your heart that God raised him from the dead, you will be saved. For it is with your heart that you believe and are justified, and it is with your mouth that you confess and are saved.* Salvation is a result of personal belief that Jesus is not only Lord of all in a general way, but also the acceptance that He will have authority over the life of each saved individual. In addition, genuine salvation is displayed through the verbal confession of the believer, accompanied by a lifestyle that reflects repentance and Christ's Lordship.

2 Corinthians 5:15: *And he died for all, that those who live should* *no longer live for themselves but for him who died for them and was raised again.* Jesus undeservedly paid the penalty for our sins, making available to each of us His gift of righteousness. As a result, those who accept His gift will choose to live for Him rather than for self.

Romans 8:38–39: *For I am convinced that neither death nor life, neither angels nor demons, neither the present nor the future, nor any powers, neither height nor depth, nor anything else in all creation, will be able to separate us from the love of God that is in Christ Jesus our Lord.* When a person accepts God's gift of grace, they can rest assured that nothing can ever separate them from the love of God because they are in Christ Jesus.

Participation in Evangelistic Endeavors

God may lead you to participate in evangelistic endeavors in which an invitation is given for people to discuss questions they have or decisions they've made in response to hearing the gospel. Since the life of a genuine disciple is based on understanding and acceptance of absolute truth, this role could have enormous spiritual significance. If you have the privilege of being placed in this position, never assume why someone is seeking counsel.

Asking a question such as "How may I help you?", rather than presuming or putting words in a person's mouth, can be helpful in determining genuine intent. There are a variety of possible responses. For instance, if the person's response reveals their desire to receive God's grace, it's important that you allow them to communicate their understanding. Replying with comments and questions such as these will prompt them to do so: "That's wonderful that you want to know Jesus. What does knowing Jesus mean to you?" Or, "What is it that made you want to accept Jesus?" Listen carefully to the person's comments and questions. Then, rely on Scripture and the leading of the Holy Spirit to patiently guide them in truth, affirming right understanding and correcting any errant thoughts.

Some people are by nature emotional. Coming to an understanding of Christ's love and forgiveness can also stir one's emotions. For these reasons, take the time to be certain that each person is basing a personal decision to follow Jesus on acceptance of biblical truth rather than on a merely emotional experience. On the other hand, some people approach a subject from a purely academic perspective. In this instance, the person considering the gospel may require more in-depth information concerning the history of God's plan of salvation and may ask for an explanation of the words used in association with the gospel. Both a history of God's plan of salvation and word definitions used when explaining salvation are included in this Appendix.

Below are effective ways to reply to other responses to the question, "How may I help you?"

Person's Response	Possible Reply
"I just came to be with my friends."	"I'm available if you want to talk."
"I just came to talk to someone."	"I'd be happy to talk with you."
"I came to pray."	"I would be happy to pray with you, if you want me to."
"I'm not sure why I came."	"Maybe I could help you figure that out."

Rededication

A person may tell you that they desire to "rededicate their life to Christ." People often use this phrase when referring to the idea that they were once living for Jesus but have strayed far from the path of righteousness and want to return to a closer relationship with Him. Since it's never God's desire for us to wander from Him, it's important that you are prepared to carefully and lovingly discuss this subject. Consider for a moment John 8:12, when Jesus said, *"I am the light of the world. Whoever follows me will never walk in darkness, but will have the light of life."* Since Jesus is the true Light, those who wholeheartedly follow Him will not persist or continue in a lifestyle that is in darkness or in opposition to His truth (1 John 1:5–7). For this reason, when a person expresses a desire for "rededication," it's important to first gain understanding of their spiritual journey.

Kindly ask the person if they would be willing to share their spiritual experience and what has led them to this current decision. As they talk, listen carefully for details concerning a professed earlier conversion, their understanding of salvation, and what may have caused them to stray from the Lord. Could it be that this person understood or even embraced part of the gospel message without personally surrendering to Jesus' authority? Have they been uninformed or misinformed concerning the truth of God's grace? Are they a true believer needing to repent of sinful behavior patterns? Rely on the Holy Spirit to reveal to you any error in their thinking.

Then, if necessary, guide them by using biblical truth to correct misguided thought patterns. Remember, a genuine turn in direction toward God occurs through repentance (Proverbs 28:13–14; Isaiah 55:7), and repentance involves a change in thought patterns that result in changed behavior. If the person tells you that there was a time in their life that they were following Christ and at some point chose to stop doing so, lovingly explain the Bible's definition of a Christ-follower and how that involves full surrender to His Lordship. If they begin questioning personal salvation and it becomes clear that they have never fully surrendered to Jesus, point them to the truth of God's grace and invite them to receive Jesus as Lord of their life. Then, encourage them to enlist in personal discipleship while pointing out the many benefits of growing in personal knowledge, understanding, and application of God's Word.

If the person shows evidence of yielding to Christ's authority, help them understand that God's gift of grace saves us and then teaches us to walk in close relationship with Him (Titus 2:11–14). Point them to 1 John 1:8–9 and encourage them to develop the habit of acknowledging personal sin through confession to God. In addition to admitting to wrongdoing, verse 9 shows that God wants us to repent and rely on His power to enable us to turn away from sinful behavior. This way of life results in continual forgiveness and purification from sin rather than a self-created pattern of "rededication."

Apart from correct application of biblical truth, a person will fail to experience long-term spiritual transformation. Assisting a person in correcting thought patterns to reflect biblical truth (thereby, promoting correct application) is one of the greatest privileges of discipleship.

Baptism

Similar to the way a photo depicts a previous experience, water baptism can be explained as a public testimony to what has already taken place in the life of a believer. Paul provides a word picture of baptism in Romans 6:3–4: *Or don't you know that all of us who were baptized into Christ Jesus were baptized into his death? We were therefore buried with him through baptism into death in order that, just as Christ was raised from the dead through the glory of the Father, we too may live a new life.* In this passage, Paul is explaining how uniting with Christ through repentance is being immersed in Him. As we choose to turn away from our old sinful nature, we identify with Christ Jesus' death. Through walking in our new nature in Jesus, we experience the same power that victoriously raised Him from the dead. Because God desires that our lives reflect His glory, He asks us to participate in water baptism as an outward testimony to His inner work (Colossians 2:11–12).

Remember our commission from Matthew 28:19: *"Therefore go and make disciples of all nations, baptizing them in the name of the Father and of the Son and of the Holy Spirit.* This verse shows that initial repentance and belief in Jesus are to precede water baptism. Therefore, the act of baptism is not necessary for salvation but is necessary for obedience (Acts 2:38, 41).

Be mindful that there may be an occasion in which a conversation reveals that a person's baptism was not based on personal faith in Jesus. In Acts 19:1–5, Luke records some men who were considered disciples yet lacked a full understanding of true salvation: *While Apollos was at Corinth, Paul took the road through the interior and arrived at Ephesus. There he found some disciples and asked them, "Did you receive the Holy Spirit when you believed?"* (Note: Genuine salvation is evidenced by the indwelling Holy Spirit. See Romans 8:9.)

They answered, "No, we have not even heard that there is a Holy Spirit." So Paul asked, "Then what baptism did you receive?" "John's baptism," they replied. Paul said, "John's baptism was a baptism of repentance. He told the people to believe in the one coming after him, that is, in Jesus." On hearing this, they were baptized into the name of the Lord Jesus.

There are several significant lessons that we can take away from this passage. First of all, rather than presume about the spiritual well-being of these men, Paul inquired of them concerning their salvation experience. Just as in this example, people today may have based their salvation on incomplete or even incorrect information. For this reason, we should take the time to lovingly and genuinely inquire, rather than merely presume, about a person's spiritual well-being.

The answers received from biblically-based questions will reveal a person's belief system, providing you with valuable insight into their level of spiritual understanding. Some people may be reluctant to ask questions of others pertaining to their salvation, believing their inquiry may be too personal, intrusive, or potentially offensive. Rather than presume you will offend, ask the Holy Spirit to lead you in asking biblically-based questions of others to better ascertain their level of spiritual understanding.

Notice that in verse 4, Paul used truth to help the men fill the gaps in their understanding and to clarify what was required for genuine salvation. He pointed these men to the saving grace of Jesus, because belief in anyone else would result in a false rather than a true conversion. Since a person will never experience victory apart from the work of the Holy Spirit, we are to follow Paul's example in communicating with others the necessary criteria for salvation.

Also, we should ask the Lord to enable us to discern those persons who may think they are saved, but may actually be lost. As you present the truth of God's Word, you may experience such an occasion in discipleship. If this situation occurs, stop and invite the person you are discipling to receive Jesus Christ by faith, accompanied by genuine repentance.

Communion

In helping believers understand the significance of Communion, it's beneficial to be able to explain its origin. In chapter 22 of Luke, we find Jesus celebrating Passover with His disciples. In verses 14–20 Luke wrote, *When the hour came, Jesus and his apostles reclined at the table. And he said to them, "I have eagerly desired to eat this Passover with you before I suffer. For I tell you, I will not eat it again until it finds fulfillment in the kingdom of God."*

After taking the cup, he gave thanks and said, "Take this and divide it among you. For I tell you I will not drink again of the fruit of the vine until the kingdom of God comes."

And he took bread, gave thanks and broke it, and gave it to them, saying, "This is my body given for you; do this in remembrance of me."

In the same way, after the supper he took the cup, saying, "This cup is the new covenant in my blood, which is poured out for you."

There are several important points that should be conveyed from this passage, especially to new believers in Jesus. First of all, Passover was celebrated to commemorate God delivering His people, the Israelites, from the bondage of slavery in Egypt (Exodus 12:14–27). From Luke 22:14–20, we see that our precious Lord Jesus, who is referred to as the perfect Passover Lamb, would soon deliver mankind from the bondage of sin. While the shed blood of animals satisfied God in the old covenant, it was incomplete for the perfect redemption of mankind. Therefore, God's plan of redemption included a new covenant. The perfectly completed work of redemption occurred in this new covenant through the shed blood of Jesus.

This is where we begin to realize the significance of Communion. The symbolic meaning of Passover was lived out through Jesus' death on the cross as His body was broken and His blood poured out for the forgiveness of sins (Matthew 26:28). This was done to fulfill the new covenant (Hebrews 7:20–22). Just as the Jewish people celebrated Passover in memory of the old covenant, disciples of Jesus observe communion as a reverent reminder of the new covenant we have in Him. In other words, Communion is the way God desires for us to acknowledge and commemorate His amazing gift of grace.

Although Jesus was not specific in how often we should partake of Communion, He did tell us to observe Communion in remembrance of Him. In doing so, we continue to proclaim the significance of His death until He comes again (1 Corinthians 11:23–26).

In addition to expressing Jesus' desire for us to participate in Communion, the Bible also teaches us the personal manner in which to observe it. As we have learned, the Lord is always most concerned with the condition of our hearts. For this reason, we should examine our hearts prior to participation in Communion, making certain we are right before Him.

If we come to His communion table with sin in our hearts, it dishonors Christ Jesus. By doing this, we would disregard the very reason we take Communion. As disciples, we are to partake in the celebration of Communion with a humble, repentant heart, motivated by respect for the life and death of our Lord Jesus (1 Corinthians 11:27–29). Train those you disciple to examine their hearts in light of the extreme cost Jesus paid for our sins. Further explain that participation in Communion should cause us to remember, once again, our humble state and continuous need for repentance.

About Carla MacLachlan

Following Matthew 28:18-20, it is Carla's desire that all people would enter into a personal relationship with Jesus Christ, and for believers to know how to live lives fully committed to Him. Carla's passion to make disciples is demonstrated in her lifestyle, writing, and teaching. Through practical application of Scripture, she equips and trains others to walk by faith and to experience the abundant life Jesus promises.

Speaking Opportunities

Carla trains others in godly living through:

- evangelism and discipleship training
- parenting seminars for parents of children of all ages
- family seminars for parents and youth
- grandparenting seminars
- college and single women's retreats
- church leadership seminars

For more information, visit **carlamaclahlan.com**,
or email i**nfo@carlamaclachlan.com**.

Other Titles by Carla

ISBN 978-0-9829029-0-5
351 PAGES, SOFTCOVER

Parenting Moment by Moment is a comprehensive manual for parenting God's way. Written in devotional form, it includes Scripture from every book in the Bible and relates principles to all ages of children, infancy through adulthood. It is encouraging to know that in the ever-changing stages of parenting you can learn to stand securely on truth. From cover to cover this book promotes reliance on the power of God's Word and the enabling of the Holy Spirit to accomplish God's will in parenting. By using its teaching, you will discover that successful spiritual training is a steady, continual process.

Each devotion will equip you as a parent to:

- grow in your knowledge and understanding of Scripture
- communicate truth consistently and effectively
- apply truth in your child's life moment by moment

Choosing to rely on God's Word and His Spirit will enable you to recognize and follow God's plan for parenting.

Available at **Amazon.com** and **boundbyfaithpublishers.com**. Download an excerpt of ***Parenting Moment by Moment*** from **carlamaclachlan.com**.